STUDY WORKBOOK FOR ISBN 978-1933039350

Mortgage Lending Home Mortgage Loan Processor Training

Library of Congress -in-Publication Data
October 2012

Mortgage Lending – Loan Processing Study Workbook for ISBN 978-1933039565

Printed in the United States of America

10 9 8 7 6 5 4 3 2 1

The enclosed material is designed for educational purposes only. Each State may have different certification and specific guidelines. Please refer to your State for additional and future information. The information contained herein is considered correct at the time of creation but laws and regulations are updated frequently and the reader assumes the responsibility for confirming current regulations and applicable data. The publisher and author make no warranty as to the success of the individuals using the training material contained herein. The publisher and author make no warranty as to any action taken by any individual completing this program. The reader is responsible for the appropriate use of the materials and information provided. This publication is designed to provide accurate and authoritative information concerning the subject matter. All material is sold with the understanding that neither the author nor the publisher guarantees the actions of any individual making use of the inclusions. Neither the author nor the publisher is rendering a legal opinion, accounting recommendation or other professional service. If legal advice or other expert assistance is desired, the services of a legal professional or other individual should be sought. The applicable federally released forms, disclosures and notices are generated from public domain. Copyright law does apply to all intellectual materials and all rights under said law are reserved b y the copyright owner.

Coursework is available at special quantity discounts to use as premiums and sales promotions within corporate or private training programs. To obtain information or inquire about availability please write to Director, PO Box 1, Hollidaysburg, PA 16648.

NOTICE

STUDY WORKBOOK FOR ISBN 978-1933039350

Mortgage Lending Home Mortgage Loan Processor Training

Flashcard Set

The flashcard set is designed to assist you in testing you retention of the materials. You should complete the coursework and then use a file card to cover the second row that contains the answers to each question. Review the questions and then check your answers.

When you feel you are ready for enhanced testing, complete the self-test segments of the workbook. Completing the self-tests without reference to the written text is the best method of assessing your knowledge base. If you are unable to answer a particular question, you should review the applicable chapter in its entirety.

What are the two classifications within the mortgage market?

- Banks and Brokerages
- Investing Pools and Individuals
- Primary Market and Secondary Market
- Banks and Savings Institutions

The two classifications within the mortgage market are the primary and the secondary mortgage market.

What is the purpose of a mortgage broker?

A Mortgage Broker acts as a liaison between the borrowers seeking mortgage funds and multiple funding sources.

What are the three most common
employment opportunities for a Loan
Processor?

- Government, Conventional, Other
- A Paper, B/C Paper, Nonconforming
- Prime, Sub-Prime, Conventional
- Bank, Brokerage, E Commute

The three most common employment
opportunities for a Loan Processor are
Bank, Brokerage, and E-Commuting.

What is a Loan Origination?

The process by which a mortgage
lender obtains a mortgage secured by
real property. An origination fee is
charged by the lender to process all
forms involved in obtaining a mortgage.

Which is not a common entity within the primary mortgage market?

- Mortgage Brokerage Office
- Mutual Savings Bank
- Credit Union
- Insurance Company

An Insurance Company is not a common entity within the primary mortgage market.

What is Freddie Mac?

Nickname for Federal Home Loan Mortgage Corp A financial corporation chartered by the federal government to buy pools of mortgages from lenders and sell securities backed by these mortgages.

What is an investing pool?

An Investing Pool is a group of smaller investors seeking a low risk, long term investment and having capital available to purchase packaged loan products.

What is Ginnie Mae?

Nickname for the Government National Mortgage Association

What is HUD?

- Homeowners Underwriting Department
- Department of Housing in Urban Developments
- Department of Housing and Urban Development
- None of the Above

HUD
Department of Housing and Urban Development

What is the purpose of the laws that govern the ethics and disclosures with which you handle loan processes?

The laws and acts governing ethics and disclosure practices are in place to protect the interest of the public and make the obtainment of housing and home mortgage funds a fair practice for all applicants.

What is PMI?

- Personal Mortgage Insurance
- Private Mortgage Insurance
- Public Mortgage Insurance
- Premium Mortgage Insurance

PMI
Private Mortgage Insurance

What is the Fair Credit Reporting Act ?

A consumer protection law that regulates the disclosure of consumer credit reports by credit reporting agencies and establishes procedures for correcting mistakes on a person's credit record.

What act assists in the prevention of discrimination against applicants?

- HMDA and ECOA
- ECOA and Fair Housing
- Fair Housing and RESPA
- RESPA and HMDA

ECOA and Fair Housing Acts assist in the prevention of discrimination against applicants.

What items are illegal for use in evaluating applicant's qualifications?

- Race, color, religion, sex, national origin, marital status, age, source of income, handicap, and familial status
- Credit, employment, mortgage or rental history, and property value
- Race, color, religion, Credit, employment, mortgage or rental history, and property value
- None of the Above

Race, color, religion, sex, national origin, marital status, age, source of income, handicap, and familial status are illegal for use in evaluating applicant's qualifications.

When must a right to cancel be provided?

- At the settlement meeting
- When a borrower refinances their primary residence
- When a borrower obtains a loan against their primary residence
- When a borrower refinances any property

A notice of the borrower's right to cancel must be provided in relationship to any credit transaction that involves a security interest in a borrower's primary residence.

Why have ethics and disclosure laws been created?

* To provide the lender with a series of practical directions
* To protect the interest of the public
* To make the obtainment of mortgage funds a fair practice
* All of the above

Ethics and disclosure laws been created to provide the lender with a series of practical directions, to protect the interest of the public, and to make the obtainment of mortgage funds a fair practice.

The Loan Processor must:

• Educate the consumer
• Act in an ethical manner
• Incorporate the required practices into their daily workload
• All of the above

The Loan Processor must educate the consumer, act in an ethical manner, and incorporate fair practices into their daily workload.

Many states have created educational and licensure requirements for lending professionals.

True
False

It is true that many states have created educational and licensure requirements for lending professionals.

In 1937, what agency was created to enable more Americans to become homeowners?

- Federal Housing Acceptance
- Federal Homeowners Association
- Federal Housing Administration
- Federal Housing Authority

In 1937, the Federal Housing Administration was created to enable more Americans to become homeowners.

HMDA requires the reporting of

- Pipeline Reports
- Loan Origination Referral Data
- Public Loan Data
- None of the Above

HMDA requires the reporting of Public Loan Data

Information for the HMDA reports should be gathered:

 At the closing table
At the time of pre-qualification
At the initial application
During post-close processes

Information for the HMDA reports should be gathered at the initial application.

HUD is a direct lender.

• True
• False

HUD is a NOT a direct lender of mortgage funds.

The automatic insurance premium cancellation requires that the principal balance of the loan fall below:

- 85%
- 82%
- 80%
- 78%

The automatic insurance premium cancellation requires that the principal balance of the loan fall below 78%.

Fair housing laws are designed to prevent

Discrimination in a credit related transaction

Discrimination in the setting of application appointments

Too many underprivileged loan disbursements

None of the above

Fair housing laws are designed to prevent discrimination in a credit related transaction.

ECOA is

- Equal Credit Origination Act
- Every Credit Opportunity Agenda
- Equal Credit Opportunity Act
- None of the Above

ECOA
Equal Credit Opportunity Act

ECOA addresses:

- Discriminatory Actions
- Predatory Lending Tactics
- Required Action Disclosures
- All of the Above

ECOA addresses Discriminatory Actions, Predatory Lending Tactics, and Required Disclosures

RESPA

- Helps consumers shop for settlement services
- Eliminates referral fees
- Requires specific borrower disclosures
- All of the above

RESPA helps consumers shop for settlement services, eliminates referral fees, and requires specific borrower disclosures

The borrower has the right to cancel any credit transaction involving their home within 3 days of the funding of the transaction.

- True
- False

TRUE - The borrower has the right to cancel any credit transaction involving their home within 3 days of the funding of the transaction.

What are Closing Costs?

Expenses incurred by buyers and sellers in transferring ownership of a property. Closing costs normally include an origination fee, an attorney's fee, taxes, escrow payments, and charges for title insurance. Lenders or Real Estate Agents provide estimates of closing costs to prospective homebuyers.

What is a settlement statement?

• HUD 1
• Statement that itemizes all closing costs payable at the closing
• Final analysis of all costs and credits applicable to the loan process
• All of the Above

A settlement statement, also termed a HUD 1 is a statement that itemizes all closing costs payable at the closing and defines the costs and credits applicable to the loan process.

Most loan inquiries are taken

- By the underwriter
- By the Loan Officer
- Over the telephone
- Both B & C

Most loan inquiries are taken by the Loan Officer over the telephone.

The pre-approval questionnaire contains

- All of the information you will need from the borrower
- Most of the information you will need for the loan application
- All of the information the underwriting team will require
- Most of the information necessary to close the loan

The pre-approval questionnaire contains most of the information you will need for the loan application.

The initial contact

- Sets the tone for your relationship with the borrower
- Is the most essential information gathering period
- Sets the loan program you will use for the borrower
- None of the above

The initial contact Sets the tone for your relationship with the borrower.

What is the essential element to gaining the information you need from a borrower?

You must ask for the information.

You may enter common nicknames
for the borrower

- True
- False

You should enter the borrower's full,
legal name. You should not use
common nicknames for the borrower.

You must always have a co-borrower
for the loan

- True
- False

FALSE – A loan application can be
made by one or more individuals.

Why do you ask if the applicant has chosen a home to purchase during the pre-qualification interview?

- So you can assess the urgency of the query
- To determine if the borrower is working with an agent thereby strengthening referral relationships
- To obtain real purchase numbers for the pre-qualification
- All of the Above

Knowing if the borrower has chosen a home at the time of the initial inquiry enables you to assess the urgency of the query, determine if the borrower is working with an agent thereby strengthening referral relationships, and obtain real purchase numbers for the pre-qualification.

Why should you request referral information of each pre-qualification?

You should request referral information from each borrower to assist in tracking referral source information, assessing marketing and advertising effectiveness and to provide follow-up information regarding the applicant to the referral source.

You should complete the pre-qualification questionnaire as soon as the borrower locates the home they wish to purchase.

- True
- False

FALSE - You should complete the pre-qualification questionnaire when the borrower makes the initial inquiry contact.

What is meant by Pre-qualification?

An early evaluation by a lender of a potential homebuyer's credit report, plus earnings, savings, and debt information. The homebuyer gets a non-binding estimate of the mortgage amount the borrower would qualify for, or how much house the borrower can afford. Buyers who pre-qualify can go a step further and seek a pre-approval.

The most important lending product is

- Low rate loans and fixed products
- Professionalism and responsiveness
- Varied products with low down payment
- None of the above

The most important lending product is the professionalism and responsiveness you bring to your customer contacts.

The pre-qualification questionnaire will provide

- answers to every question on the questionnaire
- information that will be noted in the explanation of credit section
- all of the required documentation
- none of the above

Throughout the pre-qualification questionnaire the borrower will provide you with information that will be noted in the explanation of credit section of the questionnaire.

Why would you include borrower income that cannot be used for qualifying purposes on the application?

To assist in modifying DTI Ratios
In case a compensating factor is needed
Approval levels will vary depending on the income of the borrower
Any of the Above

You would include borrower income that cannot be used for qualifying purposes on the application to bring this information to the attention of the underwriter early in the process in order to set the stage for compensating factors in the event an exception is required.

Why is it important to enter information regarding the use the borrower plans to make of the property?

- An occupancy declaration will be required at closing
- A non-owner occupied investment property requires a different application
- Approval levels will vary depending on the occupancy status
- Any of the Above

It is important to enter information regarding the use the borrower plans to make of the property because approval levels will vary depending on the occupancy status of the property.

Overtime and bonus income may be
used to qualify a borrower providing
there is:

A one-year history
A three-year history
A two-year history
A verbal history

Overtime and bonus income may be
used to qualify a borrower providing
there is a two-year history of receiving
this income.

What type of rental income is an
acceptable source of income?

- Income from roommates
- Income from boarders
- Income from an investment property
  received under a lease
- All of the Above

Rental income is an acceptable source
of income if it is from an investment
property received under a lease.

What percentage of business must a borrower own to be considered self-employed?

- 25%
- 75%
- 90%
- 85%

A borrower can be considered self-employed if they own 25% or more interest in a business.

A borrower may choose to use alimony, child support or separate maintenance if they provide what documentation?

- 12 month payment history from the courts
- Evidence that the payments will continue for at least three years
- Court documents showing who was awarded the largest portion of the overall assets
- Both A & B

A borrower may choose to use alimony, child support or separate maintenance if they provide evidence that the payments will continue for at least three years.

Employment and income do not
need to be verified for a non-
conventional loan.

- True
- False

Employment and income must be
verified on all loan programs except
light documentation programs.

If the mortgage or rental history is not included in the
credit report, which of the following is an acceptable
replacement?

- Verification forms sent to the mortgage holder or rental
  management company, if these are an entity not an
  individual to verify the history of the account

- A letter from the landlord or mortgage holder saying
  the rent or mortgage payment was received in a timely
  manner

- 12 months cancelled rent checks showing a timely
  payment to an individual landlord or mortgage holder

- Both A & C

If the mortgage or rental history is not
included in the credit report verification
forms sent to the mortgage holder or
rental management company to verify
the history of the account or 12 months
cancelled rent checks showing a timely
payment to an individual landlord or
mortgage holder is an acceptable
replacement.

Mortgage or rental history is often used to project the probability of a borrower repaying their new mortgage in a timely manner.

- True
- False

TRUE - Mortgage or rental history is often used to project the probability of a borrower repaying their new mortgage in a timely manner.

Federal Housing Acts have differing guidelines for

- Single Family Houses
- Multiple unit property
- Second Homes
- All of the above

Federal Housing Acts have differing guidelines for single family houses, multiple unit property, and second homes.

Occupancy Status will effect

• Approval Levels
• Underwriting Schedule
• Appraised Value
• All of the above

Occupancy Status will effect approval levels.

Non-qualifying income should be disclosed

• Always
• Only in compensating factor requests
• Only at the request of the borrower
• Never

Non-qualifying income should be disclosed only at the request of the borrower.

It is a portion of your job function to assist borrowers in determining the source of funds to be used in a transaction.

- True
- False

TRUE - It is a portion of your job function to assist borrowers in determining the source of funds to be used in a transaction.

What is a Pre-Approval?

This process goes a step further than pre-qualification. It means the lender has contacted the borrower's employer, bank, and other places to verify all claims of earnings and assets. In return, the borrower receives a letter stating the lender is willing to grant a mortgage for a specific amount within a limited period with the stipulation that there are no material changes to the borrower's situation.

What the most common written decision you will see from underwriting?

- Approved
- Conditional
- Denied
- Any of the Above

Underwriting may issue a determination that the application is approved, conditional, or denied.

The loan processor is the liaison between

- The borrower and underwriting
- The borrower and the loan funder
- The broker and underwriting
- The lender and the broker

The loan processor is the liaison between the borrower and underwriting.

What is Disbursement ?

The release of funds held in an escrow account.

Each time you submit a stipulation
the underwriter will

- Review the entire loan file
- Request additional documentation
- Complain about the documentation
- Request a different stipulation

Each time you submit a stipulation the
underwriter will review the entire loan
file.

If you must repeatedly return to the
borrower for additional
documentation you will gain

- Borrower loyalty
- A poor reputation
- Underwriting approval
- All of the above

If you must repeatedly return to the
borrower for additional documentation
you will gain a poor reputation.

The underwriting summary is a form of

• Checklist of Inclusions
• Guideline
• Application Overview
• None of the Above

The underwriting summary is a checklist of inclusions.

What is Closing?

The meeting at which the sale of a property is finalized. The buyer signs the lender agreement for the mortgage and pays' closing costs and escrow amounts. The buyer and seller sign documents to transfer the ownership of the property. Also known as the settlement.

When requesting an appraisal you should note

- The borrower's approval rating
- The method of billing and payment
- The title company who will close the loan
- The possibility of a field review

When requesting an appraisal you should note the method of billing and payment. The appraisal will want to collect a 'pay at the door' payment when they complete the appraisal.

The most important product a Loan Processor has available is

- Low interest rates
- Fast underwriting approvals
- Customer service skills
- The ability to relate well to borrowers

The most important product a Loan Processor has available are customer service skills. A borrower will become a repeat borrower and a referral source if you use your customer service skills to build a solid and positive relationship.

The first act you will take on a loan package is to

- Pull the credit report
- Review the application
- Complete the pre-qualification
- Send VOE/VOR/VOM forms

The first act you will take on a loan package is to complete the pre-qualification.

What is the Title Search?

A check of title records to ensure that the seller is the legal owner of a property and that there are no liens or other claims against the property.

What is a Good Faith Estimate?

A written estimate of closing costs that the lender must provide to prospective homebuyers within three days of submitting a mortgage loan application.

What is hazard insurance?

Insurance coverage that compensates for physical damage to property from natural disasters such as fire and other hazards Depending on where a piece of property is located, lenders may also require flood insurance or policies covering windstorms (hurricanes) or earthquakes.

The borrower should be informed of
the final loan specifics

- Before the closing
- The day of closing
- At the closing table
- None of the above

The borrower should be informed of the
final loan specifics before the closing.

The underwriter will review all aspects
of the file including:

- Source of down payment
- The borrower's credit history
- The borrower's compensating
  factors
- All of the above

The underwriter will review all aspects of
the file including source of down
payment, the borrower's compensating
factors, the borrower's credit history.

Prior to closing conditions must be provided to the underwriter before the loan documents can be requested.

- True
- False

TRUE – The underwriter must clear all prior to close conditions before the loan documents will be issued.

The processing stage is a stage where

- All information is verified and submitted
- Missing documentation is requested
- All loan specifics are finalized
- All of the above

The processing stage is a stage where all information is verified, documentation is submitted to underwriting, missing documentation is requested, and all loan specifics are finalized.

A verification of deposit is a form sent

- To the closing or settlement agent to verify the funds to close
- To the bank to verify the average bank account balance of the borrower
- To the real estate agent to verify the earnest money deposit
- None of the above

A verification of deposit is a form sent to the bank to verify the average bank account balance of the borrower.

What are Closing Costs?

Expenses incurred by buyers and sellers in transferring ownership of a property. Closing costs normally include an origination fee, an attorney's fee, taxes, escrow payments, and charges for title insurance. Lenders or Real Estate Agents provide estimates of closing costs to prospective homebuyers.

The funding is when

- The underwriter completes a final loan review
- The monies borrowed are wired or sent to the closing agent
- The monies borrowed are disbursed to the proper individuals
- None of the Above

The funding is when the monies borrowed are wired or sent to the closing agent.

Many loan processors forget to create

- A good closing team
- An adequate filing system
- Positive service relationships
- Borrower commitment

Many loan processors forget to create positive service relationships.

An affinity service provider includes any individual who must accomplish tasks in a timely and professional manner in order for you to accomplish your goal of closed loans.

- True
- False

TRUE - An affinity service provider includes any individual who must accomplish tasks in a timely and professional manner in order for you to accomplish your goal of closed loans.

You should treat your affinity service providers

- Respectfully
- Friendly
- With Consideration
- All of the above

You should treat your affinity service providers with respect and consideration to help foster positive affinity service relationships.

Section

2

Skill Enhancement Self-Tests

Name
Loan Processor Review Questions
Fundamentals
Instructor:
Score:

1.   What are the two classifications within the mortgage market?

_____

_____

_____

_____

_____

2.   What is an investing pool?

_____

_____

_____

_____

_____

3.   What are the three most common employment opportunities for a loan processor?

_____

_____

_____

_____

_____

_____

4.   What is the purpose of a mortgage brokerage?

_____

_____

_____

_____

_____

5.   What are the most common entities within the secondary mortgage market/

_____

_____

_____

_____

_____

6.   Which is not a common entity within the primary mortgage market?
        a.   Mortgage Brokerage Office
        b.   Mutual Savings Bank
        c.   Credit Union
        d.   Insurance Company

Name
Loan Processor Review Questions
Chapter 2 - Ethics and Disclosure
Instructor:
Score:

1.   What is the purpose of the laws that govern the ethics and disclosures with which you
        handle loan processes?

_____

_____

_____

_____

_____

_____

2.   What is HMDA?

_____

_____

_____

_____

_____

3.   What is the purpose of fair housing laws?

_____

_____

_____

_____

_____

4. What other act assists in the prevention of discrimination against applicants?

_____

_____

_____

_____

_____

5. What items are illegal for use in evaluating applicant's qualifications?

_____

_____

_____

_____

_____

6. What are the three common notices you might provide an applicant with regard to their credit application?

_____

_____

_____

_____

_____

7. What is RESPA?

_____

_____

_____

_____

_____

_____

8.   What is the disclosure notice requirement if a loan is transferred to a new servicer?

_____

_____

_____

_____

_____

9.   What is a settlement statement?

_____

_____

_____

_____

_____

10.   What is TILA?

_____

_____

_____

_____

_____

11.   When must a right to cancel be provided?

_____

_____

_____

_____

_____

12.   Explain the reason for HOEPA. _____

_____

_____

_____

_____

_____

13.   When will PMI be automatically cancelled in a normal risk mortgage? _____

_____

_____

_____

_____

_____

14.   When will PMI be automatically cancelled in a high-risk mortgage? _____

_____

_____

_____

_____

_____

15.   What is HUD and what is their function? _____

_____

_____

_____

_____

_____

16   Why have ethics and disclosure laws been created?

    a.   To provide the lender with a series of practical directions

    b.   To protect the interest of the public

    c.   To make the obtainment of mortgage funds a fair practice

    d.   All of the above

17.   The Loan Processor must:

    a.   educate the consumer

    b.   act in an ethical manner

    c.   incorporate the required practices into their daily workload

    d.   all of the above

18.   Many states have created educational and licensure requirements for lending professionals.

    a.   True

    b.   False

19.   HMDA requires the reporting of

    a.   pipeline reports

    b.   loan origination referral data

    c.   public loan data

    d.   none of the above

20.   Information for the HMDA reports should be gathered:

    a.   at the closing table

    b.   at the time of pre-qualification

    c.   at the initial application

    d.   during post-close processes

21. Fair housing laws are designed to prevent
    a. discrimination in a credit related transaction
    b. discrimination in the setting of application appointments
    c. too many underprivileged loan disbursements
    d. none of the above

22. ECOA is
    a. equal credit origination act
    b. every credit opportunity agenda
    c. equal credit opportunity act
    d. none of the above

23. ECOA addresses:
    a. discriminatory actions
    b. predatory lending tactics
    c. required action disclosures
    d. all of the above

24. RESPA
    a. Helps consumers shop for settlement services
    b. Eliminates referral fees
    c. Requires specific borrower disclosures
    d. All of the above

25. The borrower has the right to cancel any credit transaction involving their home within 3 days of the funding of the transaction.
    a. True
    b. False

26. All borrowers must purchase flood insurance
    a.   True
    b.   False

Name
Loan Processor Review Questions
Chapter 3 - Prequalification
Instructor:
Score:

1.   What is the primary reason that many loan Processorss fail to obtain the information that will be needed for a pre-qualification?

_____

_____

_____

_____

_____

_____

2.   What is the essential element to gaining the information you need from a borrower?

_____

_____

_____

_____

_____

3.   Why is the initial contact with any potential borrower important?

_____

_____

_____

_____

_____

4.   Why should you request referral information of each pre-qualification?

_____

_____

_____

_____

_____

5.   Why do you ask if the applicant has chosen a home to purchase during the pre-qualification interview?

_____

_____

_____

_____

_____

6.   What is your most important product?

_____

_____

_____

_____

_____

7.   Most loan inquiries are taken

   a.   by the underwriter

   b.   by the loan Processor

   c.   over the telephone

   d.   both b & c

8. Your most valuable tool in planning a loan strategy is
    a. customer service skills
    b. information
    c. qualification skills
    d. loan knowledge

9. The pre-approval questionnaire contains
    a. all of the information you will need from the borrower
    b. most of the information you will need for the loan application
    c. all of the information the underwriting team will require
    d. most of the information necessary to close the loan

10. The initial contact
    a. sets the tone for your relationship with the borrower
    b. is the most essential information-gathering period
    c. sets the loan program you will use for the borrower
    d. none of the above

11. You will request a credit authorization verbally before pulling borrower credit.
    a. True
    b. False

12. You may enter common nicknames for the borrower
    a. True
    b. False

13. You must always have a co-borrower for the loan
    a. True
    b. False

14. You should complete the pre-qualification questionnaire as soon as the borrower locates the home they wish to purchase

    a. True

    b. False

15. The most important lending product is

    a. low rate loans and fixed products

    b. professionalism and responsiveness

    c. varied products with low down payment

    d. none of the above

16. The pre-qualification questionnaire will provide you with

    a. answers to every question on the questionnaire

    b. information that will be noted in the explanation of credit section

    c. all of the required documentation

    d. none of the above

1.   What are the three common written decisions you will see from underwriting?

2.   What is an affinity provider?

3.   Who is ultimately responsible for the smooth process and timely closing of the loan?

4.   How can you avoid loan process delays?

5. How can you foster positive relationships with affinity service providers?

_____

_____

_____

_____

_____

6. The underwriter will review all aspects of the file including:
   a. Source of down payment
   b. The borrower's personal recommendations
   c. The borrower's professional references
   d. All of the above

7. The underwriter will review the file and issue an
   a. approval
   b. denial
   c. conditional approval
   d. Any of the above

8. Prior to closing documents must be provided to the underwriter before the loan documents can be requested.
   a. True
   b. False

9. The processing stage is a stage where
   a. all information is verified and submitted
   b. missing documentation is requested
   c. data is transferred to the underwriter
   d. all of the above

10. A verification of deposit is a form sent
    a. To the closing or settlement agent to verify the funds to close
    b. To the bank to verify the average bank account balance of the borrower
    c. to the real estate agent to verify the earnest money deposit
    d. none of the above

11. The funding is when
    a. the underwriter completes a final loan review
    b. the monies borrowed are wired or sent to the closing agent
    c. the monies borrowed are disbursed to the proper individuals
    d. none of the above

12. Delays in the loan process can be avoided by
    a. implementing a loan process follow-up and reminder system
    b. creating strong relationships with affinity service providers
    c. efficient pipeline management
    d. all of the above

13. Many loan processors forget to create
    a. a good closing team
    b. an adequate filing system
    c. positive service relationships
    d. borrower commitment

14. An affinity service provider includes any individual who must accomplish tasks in a timely and professional manner in order for you to accomplish your goal of closed loans.
    a. True
    b. False

15. You should treat your affinity service providers
    a. Respectfully
    b. Friendly
    c. With Consideration
    d. All of the above

Chapter 6 – File Documentation
Instructor:
Score:

1.   What does the mortgage or rental history tell the loan underwriter?

_____

_____

_____

_____

_____

2.   What is a VOM?

_____

_____

_____

_____

_____

3.   Why should you request all borrower documentation at the beginning of the loan process?

_____

_____

_____

_____

_____

4.   Why is it important to document each loan package you submit?

_____

_____

_____

_____

_____

5.   Why should you note any missing information on the loan cover letter that you submit with the package?

_____

_____

_____

_____

_____

6.   What is the purpose of a stipulation list?

_____

_____

_____

_____

_____

7.   Overtime and bonus income may be used to qualify a borrower providing there is:
   a.   A one-year history
   b.   A three-year history
   c.   A two-year history
   d.   A verbal history

8.   What type of rental income is an acceptable source of income?
   a.   Income from roommates
   b.   Income from boarders
   c.   Rent received by parents
   d.   Income from an investment property received under a lease

9. What percentage of business must a borrower own to be considered self-employed?
   a. 25%
   b. 75%
   c. 90%
   d. 85%

10. A borrower may choose to use alimony, child support, or separate maintenance if they provide what documentation?
    a. 12 month payment history from the courts
    b. Evidence that the payments will continue for at least three years
    c. Court documents showing who was awarded the largest portion of the overall assets
    d. Both A & B

11. Mortgage or rental history is often used to project the probability of a borrower repaying their new mortgage in a timely manner.
    a. True
    b. False

12. If the mortgage or rental history is not included in the credit report, which of the following is an acceptable replacement?
    a. Verification forms sent to the mortgage holder or rental management company, if these are an entity not an individual to verify the history of the account

    b. A letter from the landlord or mortgage holder saying the rent or mortgage payment was received in a timely manner

    c. 12 months cancelled rent checks showing a timely payment to an individual landlord or mortgage holder

    d. Both A & C

13. Bank statement as income documentation programs are typically not penalized with a higher interest or down payment requirement because the statements are considered full documentation.
    a. True
    b. False

14. An outright gift of money toward a purchase of a home is typically acceptable if it is a gift from:
    a. A charitable organization
    b. A small loan
    c. A credit card
    d. None of the above

15. The loan processor is the liaison between
    a. the borrower and the loan funder
    b. the borrower and underwriting
    c. the broker and underwriting
    d. the lender and the broker

16. Each time you submit a stipulation the underwriter will
    a. review the entire loan file
    b. request additional documentation
    c. complain about the documentation
    d. request a different stipulation

17. If you must repeatedly return to the borrower for additional documentation you will gain
    a. borrower loyalty
    b. a poor reputation
    c. underwriting approval
    d. all of the above

18. The underwriting summary is a form of
    a. checklist of inclusions
    b. guideline
    c. application overview
    d. none of the above

19. When requesting an appraisal you should note
    a. the borrowers approval rating
    b. the method of billing and payment
    c. the title company who will close the loan
    d. the possibility of a field review

20. The most important product a Loan Processor has available is
    a. low interest rates
    b. fast underwriting approvals
    c. customer service skills
    d. the ability to relate well to borrowers

21. The borrower should be informed of the final loan specifics
    a. before the closing
    b. the day of closing
    c. at the closing table
    d. none of the above

22. The loan processor should take gifts to the closing
    a. True
    b. False

23. What is automatic underwriting? _____

_____

_____

_____

_____

_____

24. What does automatic underwriting consider? _____

_____

_____

_____

_____

_____

25. What is the largest benefit of automatic underwriting from the perspective of the loan processor?

_____

_____

_____

_____

_____

26. How is this benefit accomplished?

_____

_____

_____

_____

27. What is your primary function in relationship to automatic underwriting?

_____

_____

_____

_____

_____

28. What occurs if a loan submittal is not approved through automatic underwriting?

_____

_____

_____

_____

29. Automatic underwriting negates the need for a loan processor to review the file.
    a.   True
    b.   False

30. Automatic underwriting makes its determination by reviewing
    a. Debt ratios
    b. Credit history
    c. Collateral
    d. All of the above

31. Automatic underwriting relies on
    a. Loan Processor opinion and documentation
    b. underwriting guideline matrix compared to borrower criteria
    c. historical loan performance and statistical models
    d. all of the above

32. Underwriting proceeds less smoothly through the use of automatic underwriting
    a. True
    b. False

33. Two primary focuses of automatic underwriting are:
    a. Profit and loss
    b. Speed and fairness
    c. Interest and Fees
    d. Origination closings

34. When a loan does not meet the requirements of automatic underwriting, it will be
    a. Denied
    b. Conditionally approved
    c. Submitted traditionally
    d. Altered to conform to the requirements

KEY TERMS AND DEFINITIONS

Use the knowledge you have obtained from the text to provide the definition of the terms.

1. Closing costs:

_____

_____

_____

_____

_____

_____

2. VA Mortgage:

_____

_____

_____

_____

_____

3. Amortization Schedule:

_____

_____

_____

_____

_____

4. Closing:

_____

_____

_____

_____

_____

5. Title search:

_____

_____

_____

_____

_____

6. Disbursement:

_____

_____

_____

_____

_____

7. Credit report:

_____

_____

_____

_____

_____

8. Acceleration Clause:

_____

_____

_____

_____

_____

9.   Loan-to-value (LTV) Ratio:

_____

_____

_____

_____

_____

_____

10.   Housing Expense:

_____

_____

_____

_____

_____

11.   Pre-approval:

_____

_____

_____

_____

_____

12.   Good Faith Estimate:

_____

_____

_____

_____

_____

13.   Freddie Mac:

_____

_____

_____

_____

_____

14.   Debt-to-Income Ratio:

_____

_____

_____

_____

_____

15.   Comparables:

_____

_____

_____

_____

_____

16.   RESPA:

_____

_____

_____

_____

_____

17.   Pre-qualification:

_____
_____
_____
_____
_____
_____

18.   PITI Reserves:

_____
_____
_____
_____
_____

19.   Loan Origination:

_____
_____
_____
_____
_____

20.   Hazard Insurance:

_____
_____
_____
_____
_____

21.   Ginnie Mae:

_____

_____

_____

_____

_____

_____

22.   Fair Credit Reporting Act:

_____

_____

_____

_____

_____

23.   Fannie Mae:

_____

_____

_____

_____

_____

_____

Self-Test Answer Keys

Name
Loan Processor Answer Key
Chapter 1 - The Lending Process
Instructor:
Score:

1.   What are the two classifications within the mortgage market/
            Primary Mortgage Market

      Secondary Mortgage Market

2.   What is an investing pool?

      A group of smaller investors seeking a low risk, long term investment and having capital available to purchase packaged loan products

3.   What are the three most common employment opportunities for a loan Processor?

      Bank

      Brokerage Office

      E Commute

4.   What is the purpose of a mortgage brokerage?
      To act as a liaison between the borrowers seeking mortgage funds and multiple funding sources.

5.   What are the most common entities within the secondary mortgage market/
      Insurance Companies
      Primary Lenders with excess deposits
      Pension funds
      Individual investors

6.   Which is not a common entity within the primary mortgage market?
      d.   Insurance Company

1.   What is the purpose of the laws that govern the ethics and disclosures with which you handle loan processes?

To protect the interest of the public and make the obtainment of housing and home mortgage funds a fair practice for all applicants.

2.   What is HMDA?
The home mortgage disclosure act

3.   What is the purpose of fair housing laws?
To prevent discrimination against any borrower in the sale, rental, financing, or other housing related transaction

4.   What other act assists in the prevention of discrimination against applicants?
The equal credit opportunity act

5.   What items are illegal for use in evaluating applicant's qualifications?
Race, color, religion, sex, national origin, marital status, age, source of income, handicap, and familial status

6.   What are the three common notices you might provide an applicant with regard to their credit application?
Approval, counter-offer, or denial

7.   What is RESPA?
Real Estate Settlement Procedures Act, which helps consumers shop for settlement services and eliminates referral fees that increase the costs of certain settlement services

8.   What is the disclosure notice requirement if a loan is transferred to a new servicer?
15 days

9.   What is a settlement statement?
HUD 1 is the statement that itemizes all of the closing costs payable at the closing.

10. What is TILA?
The truth-in-lending act that is part of the consumer credit protection act. The act is meant to protect and inform the consumer by requiring specific disclosures regarding the loan terms and costs.

11. When must a right to cancel be provided?
Any credit transaction that involves a security interest in a borrower's primary residence must provide the borrower with the right to rescind.

12. Explain the reason for HOEPA.
The homeowner's equity protection act is designed to protect a borrower against unfair and abusive lending tactics.

13. When will PMI be automatically cancelled in a normal risk mortgage?
When the borrower's equity position reaches 22% if the borrower is current on mortgage payments or when the borrower reaches a 22% or greater equity position and the borrower brings their mortgage obligations current.

14. When will PMI be automatically cancelled in a high-risk mortgage?
When the loan reaches a 77% LTV, or the loan reaches the half-life whichever occurs first in time.

15. Why have ethics and disclosure laws been created?

    D   All of the above

16. The loan processor must:

    D   all of the above

17 Many states have created educational and licensure requirements for lending professionals.

    A   True

18. HMDA requires the reporting of

    C   public loan data

19. Information for the HMDA reports should be gathered:

    C   at the initial application

20. Fair housing laws are designed to prevent

    A   discrimination in a credit related transaction

21 ECOA is

    C   equal credit opportunity act

22. ECOA addresses:

    D   all of the above

23. RESPA

    D   All of the above

24. The borrower has the right to cancel any credit transaction involving their home within 3 days of the funding of the transaction.

    B   False

1.   What is the primary reason that many loan Processorss fail to obtain the information that will be needed for a pre-qualification?

Because they are afraid to ask for information

2.   What is the essential element to gaining the information you need from a borrower?
You must ask for the information

3.   Why is the initial contact with any potential borrower important?
The initial contact sets the tone for the entire relationship with that borrower. Most people will make decisions concerning your professionalism and character within the first 30 seconds of contact.

4.   Why should you request referral information of each pre-qualification?
To assist in tracking referral source information, assessing marketing and advertising effectiveness and to provide follow-up information regarding the applicant to the referral source

5.   Why do you ask if the applicant has chosen a home to purchase during the pre-qualification interview?
This question enables you to assess the urgency of the query and determine if the borrower thus enabling you to prioritize the flow of work within your office.
You will also be able to determine if the borrower is working with an agent thereby strengthening referral relationships.
If the borrower has chosen a home, you will be able to use real purchase numbers to assess DTI and borrower expectations prior to the first face-to-face meeting.

6.   What is your most important product?
The professionalism, attentiveness, and responsiveness you provide to your borrowers.

7.   Most loan inquiries are taken

     D   both b & c

8.   Your most valuable tool in planning a loan strategy is

     B   information

9.   The pre-approval questionnaire contains

     B   most of the information you will need for the loan application

10. The initial contact

     A   sets the tone for your relationship with the borrower

11. You will request a credit authorization verbally before pulling borrower credit.

     B   False

12. You may enter common nicknames for the borrower

     B   False

13. You must always have a co-borrower for the loan

     B   False

14. You should complete the pre-qualification questionnaire as soon as the borrower
     locates the home they wish to purchase

     B   False

15. The most important lending product is

     B   professionalism and responsiveness

16. The pre-qualification questionnaire will provide you with

     B   information that will be noted in the explanation of credit section

1.   What are the three common written decisions you will see from underwriting?
   Approved   Everything contained within the file meets the guidelines for final approval
   Conditional   Additional documentation will be needed to ensure final loan approval
   Denied   Aspects of the file do not conform to the guidelines

2.   What is an affinity provider?
   Any individual who must complete their tasks in a timely, professional manner in order for you to accomplish your goal of closing the loan

3.   Who is ultimately responsible for the smooth process and timely closing of the loan?
   The loan processor

4.   How can you avoid loan process delays?
   By maintaining an organized flow process, using an adequate loan process follow-up and affinity service provider reminder-system.

5.   How can you foster positive relationships with affinity service providers?
   By treating these providers in a respectful, friendly, and considerate manner to foster positive relationships, build rapport and create an overall good relationship.

6.   The underwriter will review all aspects of the file including:
   D   All of the above

7.   The underwriter will review the file and issue an
   D   Any of the above

8.   Prior to closing documents must be provided to the underwriter before the loan documents can be requested.
   B   False

9.   The processing stage is a stage where
   D   all of the above

10. A verification of deposit is a form sent
     B   To the bank to verify the average bank account balance of the borrower

11. The funding is when
     B   the monies borrowed are wired or sent to the closing agent

12. Delays in the loan process can be avoided by
     D   all of the above

13. Many loan Processors forget to create
     C   positive service relationships

14. An affinity service provider includes any individual who must accomplish tasks in a
     timely and professional manner in order for you to accomplish your goal of closed
     loans.
     A   True

15. You should treat your affinity service providers
     D   All of the above

1.   What does the mortgage or rental history tell the loan underwriter?
        The probability that the borrower will repay their new mortgage in a timely manner

2.   What is a VOM?
        Verification of Mortgage

3.   Why should you request all borrower documentation at the beginning of the loan process?
        To ensure you are able to verify information, structure the loan package correctly, and request supporting information in an efficient manner.

4.   Why is it important to document each loan package you submit?
        Without proper documentation, the underwriter cannot make a valid decision on the loan package and will request additional items or stipulations prior to issuing an approval or conditional approval.

5.   Why should you note any missing information on the loan cover letter that you submit with the package?
        To assure the underwriter that you are aware of the lacking information and are working to obtain all necessary documentation.

6.   What is the purpose of a stipulation list?
        To allow the underwriter to request information required for loan decision, closing or secondary market sale and to provide clarification information regarding any file item that is unclear to the underwriter.

7.   Overtime and bonus income may be used to qualify a borrower providing there is:
        A two-year history

8.   What type of rental income is an acceptable source of income?

        D   Income from an investment property received under a lease

9. What percentage of business must a borrower own to be considered self-employed?
   A   25%

10. A borrower may choose to use alimony, child support, or separate maintenance if they provide what documentation?
   D   Both A & B

11. Mortgage or rental history is often used to project the probability of a borrower repaying their new mortgage in a timely manner.
   A   True

12. If the mortgage or rental history is not included in the credit report, which of the following is an acceptable replacement?
   D   Both A & C

13. Bank statement as income documentation programs are typically not penalized with a higher interest or down payment requirement because the statements are considered full documentation.
   B   False

14. An outright gift of money toward a purchase of a home is typically acceptable if it is a gift from:
   A   A charitable organization

15. The Loan Processor is the liaison between
   B   the borrower and underwriting

16. Each time you submit a stipulation the underwriter will
   A   review the entire loan file

17. If you must repeatedly return to the borrower for additional documentation, you will gain
   B   a poor reputation

18. The underwriting summary is a form of
   A   checklist of inclusions

19. When requesting an appraisal you should note
   B   the method of billing and payment

20. The most important product a Loan Processor has available is
    C   customer service skills

21. The borrower should be informed of the final loan specifics
    A   before the closing

22. The loan processor should take gifts to the closing
    B   False

23. What is automatic underwriting?
    A system that relies on historical loan performance and statistical models to determine whether a loan will meet the requirements of a particular purchasing entity in the secondary market

24. What does automatic underwriting consider?
    Credit history
    Collateral standards
    Debt ratio

25. What is the largest benefit of automatic underwriting from the perspective of the loan processor?
    The speed with which the processes of the loan can be completed

26. How is this benefit accomplished?
    A computer program set with specific standards and parameters compares the borrower's situation and no underwriter is required to review these specifics removing time considerations, backlog issues and human opinion.

27. What is your primary function in relationship to automatic underwriting?
    To ensure that all applications, credit reports, debt and income information and other required documentation are correctly entered into the computer.

28. What occurs if a loan submittal is not approved through automatic underwriting?
    The package is submitted to underwriting using the traditional underwriting processes.

29. Automatic underwriting negates the need for a loan processor to review the file.
    B   False

30. Automatic underwriting makes its determination by reviewing
    D   All of the above

31. Automatic underwriting relies on
    C   historical loan performance and statistical models

32. Underwriting proceeds less smoothly through the use of automatic underwriting
    B   False

33. Two primary focuses of automatic underwriting are:
    B   Speed and fairness

34. When a loan does not meet the requirements of automatic underwriting, it will be
    C   Submitted traditionally

KEY TERMS AND DEFINITIONS

1.   Closing costs:

   Expenses incurred by buyers and sellers in transferring ownership of a property. Closing costs normally include an origination fee, an attorney's fee, taxes, escrow payments, and charges for title insurance. Lenders or Real Estate Agents provide estimates of closing costs to prospective homebuyers

2.   VA Mortgage:
   A loan backed by the Veterans Administration. It requires very low or no down payments and has less stringent requirements for qualification. Members of the US armed forces are eligible for the loans under certain qualifying conditions

3.   Amortization Schedule:
   A timetable for the gradual repayment of a mortgage loan. An amortization schedule indicates the amount of each payment applied to interest and principal, and the remaining balance after each payment is made

4.   Closing:
   The meeting at which the sale of a property is finalized. The buyer signs the lender agreement for the mortgage and pays' closing costs and escrow amounts. The buyer and seller sign documents to transfer the ownership of the property. Also known as the settlement

5.   Title search:
   A check of title records to ensure that the seller is the legal owner of a property and that there are no liens or other claims against the property

6.   Disbursement:
   The release of funds held in an escrow account

7.   Credit report:
   A report on a person's credit history prepared by a credit bureau and used by a lender in determining a loan applicant's record for paying debts in a timely manner

8.   Acceleration Clause:
   The section of a mortgage document that allows the lender to speed up the   payment date in the event of default, making the entire principal amount due

9. Loan-to-value (LTV) Ratio:
The ratio of a mortgage loan amount to the property's appraised value or selling price, whichever is less. For example, if a home is sold for $100,000 and the mortgage amount is $80,000 the LTV is 80%

10. Housing Expense:
The percentage of gross monthly income that goes toward paying a Ratio mortgage or rent on a home

11. Pre-approval:
This process goes a step further than pre-qualification. It means the lender has contacted the borrower's employer, bank, and other places to verify all claims of earnings and assets. In return, the borrower receives a letter stating the lender is willing to grant a mortgage for a specific amount within a limited period with the stipulation that there are no material changes to the borrower's situation

12. Good Faith Estimate:
A written estimate of closing costs that the lender must provide to   prospective homebuyers within three days of submitting a mortgage loan application

13. Freddie Mac:
Nickname for Federal Home Loan Mortgage Corp. A financial corporation chartered by the federal government to buy pools of mortgages from lenders and sell securities backed by these mortgages

14. Debt-to-Income Ratio:
The percentage of a person's monthly earnings used to pay off all debt obligations. Lenders consider two ratios, constructed in slightly different ways. The first called the front-end ratio, the ratio of the monthly housing expenses – including principal, interest, property taxes, and insurance, (PITI) is compared to the borrower's gross, pretax monthly income. In the back-end ratio, a borrower's other debts such as auto loans and credit cards are figured in. Lenders usually consider both and set an acceptable ratio. Some lenders and some lending qualifying agencies only consider the back-end ratio

15. Comparables:
Refers to "comparable properties" which are used for comparative purposes in the appraisal process. Comps are recently sold properties that are similar in size, location, and amenities to the home for sale. Comps help an appraiser determine the fair market value of a property

16. RESPA:
Real Estate Settlement Procedures Act. A consumer protection law that requires lenders to give homebuyers advance notice of closing costs, which are payable at the closing or settlement meeting

17. Pre-qualification:
An early evaluation by a lender of a potential homebuyer's credit report, plus earnings, savings, and debt information   The homebuyer gets a non-binding estimate of the mortgage amount the borrower would qualify for, or how much house the borrower can afford. Buyers who pre-qualify can go a step further and seek a pre-approval

18. PITI Reserves:
A cash amount that a homebuyer must have on hand after making a down payment and paying all closing costs. The reserves required by a lender must equal the amount a buyer would pay for PITI for a specific number of months

19. Loan Origination:
The process by which a mortgage lender obtains a mortgage secured by real property. An origination fee is charged by the lender to process all forms involved in obtaining a mortgage

20. Hazard Insurance:
Insurance coverage that compensates for physical damage to property from natural disasters such as fire and other hazards Depending on where a piece of property is located, lenders may also require flood insurance or policies covering windstorms (hurricanes) or earthquakes

21. Ginnie Mae:
Nickname for the Government National Mortgage Association

22. Fair Credit Reporting Act:
A consumer protection law that regulates the disclosure of consumer credit reports by credit reporting agencies and establishes procedures for correcting mistakes on a person's credit record

23. Fannie Mae:
Nickname for Federal National Mortgage Association. It is a government-chartered non-bank financial services company and the nation's largest source of financing for home mortgages. It was started to make sure mortgage money is available in all areas of the country

Sample Forms

Disclosures

	face-to-face	Mail	Telephone
ECOA: When is an ap an ap?	At the time of face-to-face interview when the 1003 is completed Customers must sign the 1003 application. Check face-to-face interview in the box labeled "to be completed by interviewer" on page 3 of the 1003.	At the time, the branch or loan officer received the application. Check "by mail" in the box labeled "to be completed by interviewer" on page 3 of the 1003. Enter the date the application was received.	At the time, information for the 1003 was obtained over the telephone. Check "by telephone" in the box labeled "to be completed by interviewer" on page 3 of the 1003. Send the 1003 to the applicant for signature, along with copies of the GFE, TIL, and HUD Guide/ Compliance booklets.
		NOTE: Customers wanting to apply "by mail" must be sent a BLANK 1003 application. Mail applications would therefore normally be in the applicant's own handwriting.	Loan applications completed by the Loan Officers are never considered a mail application. Information taken from a customer over the telephone would constitute a "telephone application".
HMDA: Section X "Information for Government Monitoring Purposes"	Must be completed for all applications even an applicant is not present at the time the application is completed. Applicants do not have to provide information: they should check "I do not wish to provide this information" in the applicable section of the 1003. The Loan Officer may make a "best guess" regarding this information based on visual observation or surname. The LO should note on page 3 that information was "BVO" (based on visual observation).	Section X does not have to be completed by the applicant when they complete a mail application. It is not necessary to ask applicants for this information if the application is returned to the office with these areas blank. The Loan Officer will mark "I do not wish to provide this information" on the 1003 if the applicant did not do so. No further information is necessary.	Section X does not have to be completed by the applicant when they complete a telephone application. If the applicant does not wish to provide this information, the Loan Officer will mark "I do not wish to provide this information" on the 1003. No further information is necessary.
RESPA/TIL: Good Faith Estimate (GFE) & Truth-In-Lending Statement (TIL)	At the time of face-to-face meeting or sent within three business days of application date if prepared by the branch.	Mail within three business days of receipt of their mail application	Mail within three business days of the completion of a telephone application
CHARM: Consumer Handbook on Adjustable Rate Mortgage	Must be provided to all ARM applicants at the time of face-to-face interview	Must be mailed to all ARM applicants within three business days of receipt of mail application	Must be mailed to all ARM applicants within three business days of the completion of a telephone application
RESPA Affiliated Business Arrangement ECOA Appraisal Notice RESPA Servicing Disclosure FLOAT/LOCK FORM	Provide copy to applicants at the time of the face-to-face appearance. Applicants must sign and date an Acknowledgement illustrating that they received the applicable disclosures. You should retain copy in the loan file.	Mail to applicants with the blank application. You should include instructions to the applicant to return the signed and dated the Acknowledgement documents. Retain copy of the signed and dated Acknowledgement in loan file.	Mail to applicants along with the completed 1003, GFE, and TIL. You should include instructions to the applicant to return the signed and dated Acknowledgement documents. Retain copy of the signed and dated Acknowledgement in loan file.

2:6 Disclosure Reference Chart

SAMPLE HMDA REPORT

Applicant(s) Name_____
Loan Officer Name: _____ Lender Name: _____
Property Address: _____
Date of Application: _____

LOAN TYPE:
__1. Conventional
__2. FHA
__3. VA
__4. Other

PROPERTY TYPE:
__1. Single Family
__2. Manufactured Housing
__3. Multifamily

LOAN PURPOSE:
__1. Home Purchase
__2. Home Improvement
__3. Cash-out Refinance
__4. Rate/Term Refinance

OCCUPANCY:
__1. Owner Occupied
__2. Non-Owner Occupied

ACTION TAKEN:
__1. Loan originated
__2. Application approved but not accepted
__3. Application denied
__4. Counter-offer denied
__5. Application withdrawn by applicant

APPLICATION TYPE:
__1. By Mail
__2. By Phone
__3. Face-to-Face
__4. Internet

REASONS FOR DENIAL:
__1. Excessive Debt to income ratio
__2. Insufficient Employment history
__3. Credit history
__4. Collateral
__5. Insufficient cash available
__6. Other _____

2:1 Sample Form – HMDA – HUD Release Continued

FINANCIAL DISCRIMINATION ACT
FAIR LENIDNG NOTICE

It is illegal to discriminate based on

1. Trends, characteristics, or conditions in a neighborhood unless the financial institution is able to demonstrate that such consideration is required to ensure safety

2. Race, color, religion, sex, marital status, familial status, national origin, ancestry, or handicap

3.

It is illegal to consider the racial, ethnic, religious, or national origin composition of a neighborhood or geographic area surrounding a housing accommodation or whether such composition is undergoing change.

These provisions govern financial assistance for the purpose of purchase, construction, rehabilitation, or refinancing of one to four unit residences occupied by the owner.

If you have any questions about your rights, or if you wish to file a complaint you may contact:

I/we acknowledge that we received a copy of this notice:

_____   _____
Borrower Signature   Date

_____   _____
Co-Borrower Signature   Date

2:2 Sample Form – Financial Discrimination Act Fair Lending Notice – HUD Release

Federal Equal Credit Opportunity Act Notice

The Federal Equal Credit Opportunity Act prohibits creditors from discriminating against credit applicants on the basis of color, religion, national origin, sex, marital status, age (provided the applicant has the capacity to enter into a binding contract), because all of part of the applicant's income is derived from public assistance programs, or because the applicant has in good faith exercised any right under the Consumer Protection Act
Lending institutions are prohibited from bringing up certain specific subjects that lend themselves to discrimination. These subjects are as follows:

Whether or not an applicant has or will have children.

Whether or not there exist childcare problems.

Whether or not there will be interruptions of income due to childbirth.

Whether or not an applicant is receiving alimony, child support, or separate maintenance unless this income is voluntarily disclosed as a source of additional income to be considered as part of the credit application

Whether an applicant is widowed, divorced, or single

Whether or not an applicant's telephone number is publicly listed

Lending institutions must take and report actions taken on your applications within a reasonable time. If the application is denied, the reason for the denial must be provided if requested.

I/we acknowledge that we received a copy of this notice:

_____   _____
Borrower Signature   Date

_____   _____
Co-Borrower Signature   Date

2:3 Sample Form – Federal Equal Credit Opportunity Act Notice – HUD Release

Credit Information Disclosure Authorization

I / We _____ hereby authorize you to release to
_____ information for verification purposes.

This information may include:

      Employment information including past and present employers

      Banking and Savings Account Records

      Mortgage Loan Rating Information

      Rental History Information

      A consumer credit report from a credit-reporting agency

This information is for the confidential use in processing an application for a real estate loan.

A copy of this authorization and applicable signature(s) may be deemed the equivalent of the original.

_____   _____
Borrower Signature   Social Security Number

_____   _____
Print Name   Date

_____   _____
Co-Borrower Signature   Social Security Number

_____   _____
Print Name   Date

2:4 Sample Form – Credit Information Disclosure Authorization – HUD Release

CREDIT BUREAU NOTICE TO THE HOME APPLICANT

Trans Union Corporation (Empirica)

_____
Current Score   Date of Score

_____
Range of Score

Key Factors:

Equifax Information Services (Beacon)

_____
Current Score   Date of Score

_____
Range of Score

Key Factors:

Exprian Information Services (Fair Isaac)

_____
Current Score   Date of Score

_____
Range of Score

Key Factors:

In connection with your application for a home loan, we must disclose to you the score that a credit bureau distributed to users and in connection with your home loan and the key factors affecting your credit score.

The credit score is a computer-generated summary calculated at the time of the request and based on information a credit bureau or lender has on file. The scores are based on data about your credit history and payment patterns. Credit scores are important because they are used to assist the lender in determining whether you will obtain a loan. They may also be used to determine what interest rate may be offered on the mortgage. Credit scores can change over time, depending on your conduct, how your credit history and payment patterns change, and how credit-scoring technologies change.

Because the score is based on information in your credit history, it is very important that you review the credit-related information that is being furnished to make sure it is accurate. Credit records may vary from one company to another.

If you have questions about your credit score or the credit information that is furnished to you, contact the credit bureau at the address and telephone number provided.

The credit bureau plays no part in the decision to take action on the loan application and is unable to provide you with specific reasons for the decision on a loan application.

If you have questions concerning your loan, , contact

2:5 Sample Form – Credit Bureau Notice to the Home Applicant – HUD Release

Lender:	Sales Price:
Address:	Base Loan Amount:
	Total Loan Amount:
Applicant(s):	Interest Rate:
	Type of Loan:
Property Address:	Preparation Date:
	Loan Number

The information provided below reflects estimates of the charges which you are likely to incur at the settlement of your loan. The fees listed are estimates – actual charges may be more or less. Your transaction may not involve a fee for every item listed.
THE NUMBERS LISTED BESIDE THE ESTIMATES GENERALLY CORRESPOND TO THE NUMBERED LINES CONTAINED THE HUD-1 OR HUD-1A SETTLEMENT STATEMENT WHICH YOU WILL BE RECEIVEING AT THE SETTLEMENT. THE HUD-1 OR HUD-1A SETTLEMENT STATEMENT WILL SHOW YOU THE ACTUAL COST FOR ITEMS PAID AT SETTLEMENT.

800	ITEMS PAYABLE IN CONNECTION WITH LOAN;		1100	TITLE CHARGES	
801	Origination Fee @ % + $	$_____	1101	Closing or Escrow Fee	$_____
802	Discount Fee @ %+$	$_____	1102	Abstract or Title Search	$_____
803	Appraisal Fee	$_____	1103	Title Examination	$_____
804	Credit Report	$_____	1105	Document Preparation Fee	$_____
805	Lender's Inspection Fee	$_____	1106	Notary Fee	$_____
806	Mortgage Insurance Application Fee	$_____	1107	Attorney's Fee	$_____
807	Assumption Fee	$_____	1108	Title Insurance	$_____
808	Mortgage Broker Fee	$_____			$_____
810	Tax Related Service Fee	$_____			$_____
811	Application Fee	$_____			$_____
812	Commitment Fee	$_____			$_____
813	Lender's Rate Lock-In Fee	$_____			$_____
814	Processing Fee	$_____			$_____
815	Underwriting Fee	$_____			$_____
816	Wire Transfer Fee	$_____			$_____

900	ITEMS TO BE PAI DIN ADVANCE ;		1200	GOVERNMENT RECORDING AND TRANSFER CHARGES	
901	Interest for 1 days @ $13.78 day	$_____	1201	Recording Fee	$_____
902	Mortgage Insurance Premium	$_____	1202	City/County Tax/Stamps	$_____
903	Hazard Insurance Premium	$_____	1203	State Tax/Stamps	$_____
904	County Property Taxes	$_____	1205	Intangible Tax	$_____
905	Flood Insurance	$_____			$_____
		$_____			$_____

1000	RESERVES DEPOSITED WITH LENDER		1300	ADDITIONAL SETTLEMENT CHARGES	
1001	Hazard Ins 3 Mo @ $ 35 Per Mo	$_____	1201	Survey	$_____
1002	Mortgage Ins. Mo@$ Per Mo	$_____	1202	Pest Inspection	$_____
1004	Tax & Assmt. 7 Mo@$110 Per Mo	$_____	1203		$_____
1006	Flood Insurance	$_____	1205		$_____
		$_____		TOTAL ESTIMATED SETTLMENT CHARGES $_____	

S/B designates these costs to be paid by Seller / Broker   A designates those costs effecting APR

TOTAL ESTIMATED MONTHLY PAYMENT		TOTAL ESTIMATED FUNDS TO CLOSE	
Principal & Interest	$_____		
Real Estate Taxes	$_____	Down Payment	$_____
Hazard Insurance	$_____	Estimated Closing Costs (not financed)	$_____
Flood Insurance	$_____	Estimated Prepaid Items/Reserves	$_____
Mortgage Insurance	$_____	Total Paid Items (subtract)	$_____
Other	$_____	Other	$_____
TOTAL MONTHLY PAYMENT	$_____	CASH FROM BORROWER	$_____

2:7 Sample Form – Good Faith Estimate – HUD Release

APPROVED SERVICE PROVIDER LIST

Addendum to the standard "Good Faith Estimate" of Settlement Costs

_____ requires the use of certain providers in the processing and settlement of your loan. These providers are chosen from an approved list and we require that you pay for all portions of the services provided from these providers. The costs of these services are based on the charges of these providers or industry standards. Please refer to your attached Good Faith Estimate form for an estimate of each proposed charge. The following providers have been repeatedly used for the designated services within the last 12 months.

1.   CREDIT REPORTING AGENCIES:

2.   APPRAISAL SERVICES:

3.   PRIVATE MORTGAGE INSURANCE PROVIDERS:

4.   OTHER:

I/we acknowledge that we received a copy of this notice:

_____   _____
Borrower Signature   Date

_____   _____
Co-Borrower Signature   Date

2:12 Sample Form– Approved Service Provider List – HUD Release

RATE LOCK/RATE FLOAT OPTION

Loan Amount $ _____

Property Address _____

City, State, Zip _____

This is to certify that I DO want to exercise my interest rate lock option at this time.

A.   My guaranteed interest rate will be _____%.

B.   The total points paid at settlement will not exceed _____. This total does not include settlement costs such as title insurance, homeowners insurance, transfer taxes, etc.

C.

D.   This agreement will end _____ days from today. This date is called the ending date.

ACKNOWLEDGEMENT

_____   _____
Signed   Date

This is to certify that I DO NOT want to exercise my interest rate lock option at this time.

A.   I understand that my lender cannot predict interest rate changes.

B.   If I want to obtain an interest rate commitment in the future, I may do so at any time up to ____ days before the closing of my mortgage loan.

C.   I understand that I must sign an interest rate lock-in agreement to obtain a guaranteed interest rate lock.

D.   I understand that it is my responsibility to advise the lender of my desire to obtain interest rate commitment.

ACKNOWLEDGEMENT

_____   _____
Signed   Date

_____   _____
Signed   Date

Affiliated Business Arrangement Notice

This is to give you notice that _____ has a business relationship with _____

(Describe the nature of the relationship between the referring party and the provider(s). Including percentage of ownership interest, if applicable). Because of this relationship, this referral may provide a financial or other benefit.

(A.) Set forth below is the estimated charge or range of charges for the settlement services listed. You are NOT required to use the listed provider(s) as a condition for (settlement of your loan) (or) (purchase, sale or refinance of) the subject property. THERE ARE FREQUENTLY OTHER SETTLEMENT SERVICE PROVIDERS AVAILABLE WITH SIMILAR SERVICES. YOU ARE FREE TO SHOP AROUND TO DETERMINE THAT YOU ARE RECEIVING THE BEST RATE FOR THESE SERVICES.

_____

_____

(B.) Set forth below is the estimated charge or range of charges for the settlement services of an attorney, credit reporting agency, or real estate appraiser that we, as your lender, will require you to use, as a condition of your loan on this property, to represent our interests in this transaction.

_____

_____

ACKNOWLEDGMENT

I/we have read this disclosure form and understand that (referring party) is referring me/us to purchase the above described settlement service(s) and may receive a financial benefit as a result of this referral.

_____   _____

MAILING ADDRESS CONFIRMATION / PAYMENT LETTER

From:

Re: Loan #   *** IMPORTANT, PLEASE READ THROUGHOULY ***
        Property Address

To:

Dear Homeowner:

A.   All mortgage servicing correspondence will be mailed to the above referenced property address. In order to
ensure proper   receipt of all mortgage servicing notifications (i.e. monthly statement, Q&A booklets, etc.) please
indicate the correct mailing address if it is different from the property address. The address to mail payments and the phone
number to call   for customer service are listed below.

        Please indicate (X):

        ( )   The property address is correct as referenced above and should be used for correspondence.

        ( )   The proper mailing address is: _____

                                                     _____

B..   The monthly payments on the above loan are to begin on   , and will continue
monthly until

        Your monthly payment will consist of the following:

        MONTHLY PAYMENT …………………………………………$_____
        MMI/PMI INSRUANCE ………………………………………….. _____
        RESERVE FOR COUNTY TAXES ………………………………. _____
        RESERVE FOR HAXARD INSURANCE…………………………… _____
        RESERVE FOR FLOOD INSURANCE………………………………. _____
        RESERVE FOR CITY TAXES……………………………………._____
        RESERVE FOR ANNUAL ASSESSMENT…………………………._____
        RESERVE FOR SCHOOL TAXES………………………………….._____
        _____..................................
                        TOTAL MONTHLY PAYMENTS……….$_____

*** Please be aware that if you have an impound account, you may see a change in your initial monthly payment figure due
to information available after the closing of your loan.

                        Engages the services of   as its servicer. You will be receiving a
billing notice from   within two weeks of your loan funding.   has the
right to collect your payments and this in no way affects the terms and conditions of the mortgage instruments, other than
the terms directly related to the servicing of your loan. If you do not receive a payment booklet or have other questions
about the servicing of your loan, please call:

Mortgage Servicing Disclosure

NOTICE TO MORTGAGE LOAN APPLICATNS: THE RIGHT TO COLLECT YOUR MORTGAGE LOAN PAYMENTS MAY BE TRANSFERRED. FEDERAL LAW GIVES YOU CERTAIN RELATED RIGHTS. READ THIS STATEMTN AND SIGN IT ONLY IF YOU UNDERSTAND ITS CONTENTS.

Because you are applying for a mortgage loan covered by the Real Estate Settlement Procedures Act (RESPA), you have certain rights under that Federal law. This statement tells you about those rights. It also tells you what the chances are that the servicing for this loan may be transferred to a different loan servicer. "Servicing" refers to collecting your principal, interest and escrow account payments, if any. If your loan servicer changes, certain procedures must be followed. This statement generally explains those procedures.

Transfer Practices and Requirements

If the servicing of your loan is assigned, sold or transferred to a new servicer you must be given notice of that transfer. The present loan servicer must send you notice in writing of the assignment, sale, or transfer of the servicing not less than 15 days before the effective date of the transfer. The present servicer and the new servicer may combine this information in one notice so long as the notice is sent to you within 15 days before the effective date of the transfer. The 15-day period is not applicable if a notice of prospective transfer is provided to you at settlement. The law allows a delay in the time (not more than 30 days after a transfer) for servicers to notify you under certain limited circumstances, when your servicer is changed abruptly. This exception applies only if your servicer is fired for cause, is in bankruptcy proceedings, or is involved in a conservatorship or receivership initiated by a Federal Agency.

Notices must contain certain information. They must contain the effective date of the transfer of the servicing of your loan to the new servicer, the name, address and toll-free or collect call telephone number of the new servicer, and toll-free or collect call telephone numbers of a person or department for both your present servicer and your new servicer to answer your questions about the transfer of servicing. During the 60-day period following the effective date of the transfer of the loan servicing, a loan payment received by your old servicer before its due date may not be treated by the new servicer as late and a late fee may not be imposed on you.

Complaint Resolution

Section 5 of RESPA gives you certain consumer rights *whether or not your loan servicing is transferred.* If you send a qualified written request to your loan servicer concerning the servicing of your loan, your servicer must provide you with a written acknowledgement within 20 business days of receipt of your request. A "qualified written request" is a written correspondence other than notice on payment coupon or other payment medium supplied by the servicer that includes your name and account number and your reasons for the request. Not later than 60 Business Days after receiving your request, your servicer must make any appropriate corrections to your account or must provide you with a written clarification regarding any dispute. During this 60-Business Day period, your servicer may not provide any information to a consumer reporting agency concerning any overdue payment related to such period or qualified written request.

A business day is any day excluding public holidays, State or Federal, Saturday or Sunday.

Damages and Costs

Section 6 of RESPA also provides for damages and costs for individuals in circumstances where servicers are shown to have violated the requirements of that section.

Servicing Transfer Estimated by Lender

1. The following is the best estimate of what will happen to the servicing of your loan:
    We may assign, sell, or transfer the servicing of your loan sometime while the loan is outstanding. We are able to service your loan and we presently intend to service your loan.

2. For all mortgage loans that we make in the 12-month period after your mortgage loan is funded, we estimate that the percentage of mortgage loans for which we will transfer servicing is between:
    ___ and ___%

    This is only our best estimate and it is not binding. Business conditions or other circumstances may affect

3. This is our record of transferring the servicing of mortgage loans we have made in the past:
    Year   Percentage of Loans Transferred

ACKNOWLEDGEMENT OF MORTGAGE LOAN APPLICANT

I/We have read this disclosure form and understand the contents as evidenced by my/our signature(s) below. I/We understand that this acknowledgement is a required part of the mortgage loan application.

2:16 Sample Form – Mortgage Servicing Disclosure – HUD Release

NOTICE REGARDING YOUR

UNIFORM RESIDENTIAL APPRAISAL REPORT

You are advised that you have the right, under the Equal Credit Opportunity Act, to obtain a copy of your *Uniform Residential Appraisal Report*.

If you wish a copy, please write us at the address shown below. We must hear from you no later than 90 days after we notify you about the action taken on your credit application or you withdraw your application.

Please send your written request to:

In your letter, give the following information:

> *Loan or application number (if known)*
> *Date of application*
> *Name(s) of loan applicant(s)*
> *Property address*
> *Current mailing address*

A copy of your Uniform Residential Appraisal Report shall be mailed to you within 30 days after receipt of your request.

Please acknowledge receipt of this Notice by signing and dating below.

_____   _____
Borrower   Co-Borrower

2:17 Sample Form – Right to Receive a Copy of Appraisal – HUD Release

NOTICE OF RIGHT TO CANCEL

Your Right to Cancel

You are entering a transaction that will result in a mortgage on your home. You have a legal right under Federal Law to cancel this transaction without cost until midnight of the third business day after, whichever of the following events occurs last

      (1.)   the date of the closing of the transaction
      (2.)   the date you received your Truth in Lending disclosure
      (3.)   the date you received this notice of your right to cancel

If you cancel the transaction, the mortgage is also canceled. Within 20 calendar days after we receive your notice
we must take the steps necessary to reflect the fact that the mortgage on your house has been cancelled, and we must return to you any money or property you have given to us or to anyone else in connection with this transaction.

You may keep any money or property we have given you until we have completed the items mentioned above, but you must return the money or property upon completion of the described actions. If it is impractical or unfair for you to return the property, you must offer its reasonable value. You may offer to return the property at your home or at the location of the property. Money must be returned to the address below. If we do not take possession of the money or property within 20 calendar days of your offer, you may keep it without further obligation.

How to Cancel

If you decide to cancel this transaction you may do so by notifying

_____

_____

You may use any written statement that is signed and dated by you and states your intention to cancel, or you may use this notice by dating and signing below. Keep one copy of this notice because it contains important information about your rights.

If you cancel by mail, you must send the notice no later than midnight of _____, 20___ (or midnight of the third business day following the latest of the events listed above.) If you send or deliver your written notice to cancel in some other manner, it must be delivered to the above address no later than that time.

ACKNOWLEDGMENT

I/we have read this disclosure form and acknowledge that we have received a copy of this notice.

2:18 Sample Form –Notice of Right to Cancel – HUD Release

F. Type of Loan				
1__ FHA 2 __ FmHA 3__ Conv 4 __ VA 5 __ Conv Ins	6. File Number:		7. Loan Number:	8. Mortgage Insurance Case Number

G. Note: This form is furnished to give you a statement of actual settlement costs. Amounts paid to and by the settlement agent are shown. Items marked "(P&C)" were paid outside the closing; they are shown here for informational purposes and are not included in the totals.

D. Name & Address of Borrower.	E. Name & Address of Seller	F. Name & Address of Lender
G. Property Location	H. Settlement Agent	I. Settlement Date
	Place of Settlement:	

J. Summary of Borrower's Transaction		K. Summary of Seller's Transaction	
100. Gross Amount Due From Borrower		**400. Gross Amount Due To Seller**	
101. Contract Sales Price		401. Contact Sales Price	
102. Personal Property		402. Personal Property	
103. Settlement Charges to borrower (line 1400)		403.	
104.		404.	
105.		405.	
Adjustments for items paid by seller in advance		Adjustments for items paid by seller in advance	
106. City / Town Taxes for		406. City / Town Taxes for	
107. County Taxes for		407. County Taxes for	
108. Assessments for		408. Assessments for	
109.		409.	
110.		410.	
111.		411.	
112.		412.	
120. Gross Amount Due From Borrower		**420. Gross Amount Due To Seller**	
200. Amounts Paid By Or In Behalf Of Borrower		**500. Reductions In Amount Due To Seller**	
201. Deposit or earnest money		501. Excess deposit (see instructions)	
202. Principal amount of new loan(s)		502. Settlement charges to seller (line 1400)	
203. Existing loan(s) take subject to		503. Existing loan(s) taken subject to	
204.		504. Payoff of first mortgage loan	
205.		505. Pay off of second mortgage loan	
206.		506.	
207.		507.	
208.		508.	
209.		509.	
Adjustments for items unpaid by seller		Adjustments for items unpaid by seller	
210. City / Town Taxes for		510. City / Town Taxes for	
211. County Taxes for		511. County Taxes for	
212. Assessments for		512. Assessments for	
213.		513.	
214.		514.	
215.		515.	
216.		516.	
217.		517.	
218.		518.	
219.		519.	
220. Total Paid By/For Borrower		**520. Total Reduction Amount Due Seller**	
300. Cash At Settlement From/To Borrower		**600. Cash at Settlement To/From Seller**	
301. Gross amount due from borrower (line 120)		601. Gross amount due to seller (line 420)	
302. Less amounts paid by/for borrower (line 220)	( )	602. Less reductions in amt due seller (line 520)	( )

	Paid From Borrowers Funds at Settlement	Paid From Seller's Funds at Settlement
700. Total Sales/Brokers commission based on price $ @ %		
Division of Commission (line 700) as follows:		
701. $ to		
702. $ to		
703 Commission paid at Settlement		
704.		
800. Items Payable in Connection with Loan		
801. Loan Origination Fee %		
802. Loan Discount %		
803. Appraisal Fee to		
804. Credit Report to		
805. Lender's Inspection Fee		
806. Mortgage Insurance Application Fee to		
807. Assumption Fee		
808.		
809.		
810.		
811.		
900. Items Required By Lender To Be Paid In Advance		
901. Interest from to @$ / day		
902. Mortgage Insurance Premium for months to		
903. Hazard Insurance Premium for years to		
904.		
905.		
1000. Reserves Deposited With Lender		
1001. Hazard Insurance months @$ per month		
1002. Mortgage Insurance months @$ per month		
1003. City Property Taxes months @$ per month		
1004. County Property Taxes months @$ per month		
1005. Annual Assessments months @$ per month		
1006. months @$ per month		
1007. months @$ per month		
1008. months @$ per month		
1100. Title Charges		
1101. Settlement or closing fee to		
1102. Abstract or title search to		
1103. Title examination to		
1104. Title insurance binder to		
1105. Document preparation to		
1106. Notary fees to		
1107. Attorney's fees to		
(includes above items numbers:)		
1108. Title Insurance to		
(includes above items numbers:)		
1109. Lender's coverage $		
1110. Owner's coverage $		
1111.		
1112.		
1200. Government Recording and Transfer Charges		
1201. Recording fees: Deed $: Mortgage $: Releases $		
1202. City/county tax/stamps: Deed $: Mortgage $		
1203. State tax/stamps: Deed $: Mortgage $		
1204.		
1205.		
1300. Additional Settlement Charges		
1301. Survey to		
1302. Pest Inspection to		
1303.		
1304.		
1305.		
1400. Total Settlement Charges (enter on lines 103, Section J and 502, Section K)		

BORROWER(S):

PROPERTY ADDRES:

NON IMPOUND NOTICE

I DO UNDERSTAND THAT THE LENDER FOR THIS MORTGAGE WILL NOT
IMPOUND FOR REAL ESTATE TAXES AND HOMEOWNERS INSURANCE
COVERAGE ON THE ABOVE REFERENCED ACCOUNT.

THE MONTHLY PAYMENT I WILL BE MAKING ONLY COVERS PRINCIPAL AND
INTEREST ON THE LOAN.

I AM FULLY RESPONSIBLE TO PAY FOR REAL ESTATE TAXES AND
HOMEOWNERS INSURACE POLICY PREMIUMS WHEN THEY BECOME
PAYABLE.

2:21 Sample Form – Non Impound Notice – HUD Release

INITIAL ESCROW ACCOUNT DISCLOSURE STATEMENT

Borrower Name and Address	Lender's Name and Address
Loan No.	Telephone No.

___ *Your mortgage payment for the coming year will be $_____ of which $_____ will be for principal and interest and $_____ will go into your escrow account.*

___ *Your first monthly mortgage payment for the coming year will be $_____ of which $_____ will be for principal and interest and $_____ will go into your escrow account.*

The terms of your loan may result in changes to the principal and interest payments during the year.

This is an estimate of activity in your escrow account during the coming year based on payments anticipated to be made from your account.

Month/ Payment No.	Payments to Escrow Acct.	Payment from Escrow Acct.	Description	Escrow Acct. Balance

Please keep this statement for comparison with the actual activity in your account at the end of the escrow accounting computation year. Cushion selected by the servicer is $_____.

2:22 Sample Form – Initial Escrow Account Disclosure Statement – HUD Release

ADJUSTABLE RATE MORTGAGE DISCLOSURE STATEMENT

IMPORTANT MORTGAGE LOAN INFORMATION - PLEASE READ CAREFULLY

PROGRAM NAME: _____

You have expressed an interest in applying for an Adjustable Rate Mortgage loan (ARM). This disclosure contains information regarding the differences between this ARM and other mortgage loans. This disclosure describes the features of the specific ARM that you are considering. Upon request, we will provide you with information about any other Adjustable Rate Mortgage programs we have available.

ADJUSTABLE RATE MORTGAGE LOAN: This loan is an Adjustable Rate Mortgage loan. The interest rate may change based upon movements of a specific interest rate index. Changes in the interest rate will be reflected by increases or decreases in the amount of your payments. The date or dates on which changes can occur will be specified in the ARM loan documents. This ARM is based on the terms and conditions of the program in which you have expressed an interest. We have based this disclosure on recent interest rates, index and margin values, and fees.

THIS DISCLOSURE: This disclosure is not a contract or loan commitment. The matters discussed in this disclosure are subject to change by us at any time without notice. DETERMINING THE INTEREST RATE: Your interest rate will be determined by means of an index that is subject to change.

> Your interest rate is based on the Index value plus a margin. A change in the index generally will result in a change in the interest rate. If the Index rate change since the previous adjustment is less than _____, the interest rate will not change. The amount that your interest rate change may also be affected by periodic interest rate change limitations and the lifetime interest rate limits set forth in your loan program.

> Interest Rate Adjustments Your interest rate under this ARM can change every _____ years.

> Your interest rate cannot increase or decrease more than _____ percentage points at each adjustment.

> Your interest rate cannot increase or decrease more than _____percentage points over the term of your loan.

> Rate adjustments under this ARM will be reflected in higher or lower payments.

DETERMINING THE PAYMENTS: Your initial monthly payment of principal and interest will be determined based on the interest rate, loan term, and loan balance when your loan is closed. Your payment will be set to amortize the loan over a period of ___ payments.

> Frequency of Payment Changes: Based on increases or decreases in the Index, payment amounts under this ARM loan can change every _____ years. Your monthly payment amount could change more frequently if there is a change in other loan factors not relating to the ARM. These factors may include taxes, assessments, insurance premiums, or other charges required when creating an escrow or impound account.

> Limitations on Payment Changes: Your payment can change every ___ years based on changes in the interest rate, loan term, or loan balance.

> Adjustment Notices: You will be notified if interest rate changes occur. If an interest rate change effects your monthly payment, you will be notified at least 25 calendar days before the changed payment is due. The notice will indicate the adjusted payment amount, interest rate, Index value, and the outstanding loan balance at that time.

** INSERT AN EXAMPLE AND INDEX TABLES AS THEY APPLY TO THE ARM UNDER DISCUSSION.

I/we acknowledge that we have received a copy of this disclosure:

Borrower Signature   Date   Co-Borrower Signature   Date

_____   _____   _____   _____

PRIVATE MORTGAGE INSURANCE INITIAL DISCLOSURE

Borrower:_____ Co-Borrower:_____

Property Address:_____

PRIVATE MORTGAGE INSURANCE TERMINATION DISCLOSURE

We <u>SAMPLE MORTGAGE COMPANY</u> require that you <u>BORROWER NAME</u> maintain private mortgage insurance ("PMI") in connection with your mortgage loan. PMI protects lenders and others against financial loss in case of borrower default. Federal law provides you with the right to cancel PMI under certain circumstances. Federal law establishes when PMI must be terminated. This Disclosure describes those cancellation and termination rights.

___1.   We have provided you with an initial amortization schedule. Federal Law basis the cancellation and termination terms on this initial amortization schedule.

___2.   Borrower Initiated Cancellation: A borrower may initiate cancellation if certain requirements are satisfied.

Term Requirements of Cancellation:

You have the right to request cancellation of PMI at any time on or after:

The date that the principal balance of the loan, based on the initial amortization schedule, reaches 80% of the original value (lesser of sales price or appraised value) of the property securing the loan.

The date that the principal balance of the loan, based on actual payments made, reaches 80% of the original value (lesser of the sales price or appraised value) of the property securing the loan.

Status Requirements for Cancellation:

PMI may be cancelled when you reach the stated percentage if you meet all of the following requirements:

You must submit your cancellation request in writing to the servicer of your loan.

You must have a good payment history on your loan.

A good payment history is described as a history where you have not made a mortgage payment that was 60 days or longer past due during the 24 months preceding the cancellation date.

The description of a good payment history also requires you have not made a mortgage payment that was 30 days or longer past due during the 12 months proceeding the cancellation date.

You must have provided the note holder with

Evidence that the value of the property securing the not has not declined below its original value.

Certification that you do not have a subordinate lien on the equity in the property

___3.   Automatic Termination: If mortgage loan payments are current, PMI will automatically terminate when the principal balance of the loan is scheduled to reach 78% of the original value (lesser of sales price or appraised value) of the property based on the initial amortization schedule.

The loan servicer will notify you when the automatic cancellation of PMI occurs.

___4.   Exemptions

There are certain exemptions to the right to cancellation and automatic termination of PMI. These exemptions relate to certain mortgage loans with higher risks associated with the extension of credit. These exemptions do not apply to your loan transaction.

I/We have received a copy of this Private Mortgage Insurance Termination Disclosure.

2:25 Sample Form – Private Mortgage Insurance Initial Disclosure – HUD Release

NOTICE OF SPECIAL FLOOD HAZARDS
NOTICE OF AVAILABILITY OF FEDERAL DISASTER RELIEF ASSISTANCE

The property securing the loan for which you have applied is located in an area identified as having special flood hazards.

The area is identified by FEMA as a special flood hazard area using FEMA's Flood Insurance Rate Map or the Flood Hazard Boundary Map for the following community:

This area has at least a one- percent chance of a flood equal to or exceeding the base flood elevation or 100-year flood plain in any given year. During the live of a 30-year mortgage loan, the risk of a 100-year flood in a special, flood hazard area is twenty-six percent.

Federal law allows the lender and the borrower to request the Director of FEMA to review the determination of the location as a special, flood hazard area. If you would like to make such a request please contact our offices at The community in which the property is located participates in the National Flood Insurance Program (NFIP). Federal law does not allow us to make the loan you have applied for if you do not purchase flood insurance. The flood insurance purchased must be maintained for the life of the loan. If you fail to purchase or renew the flood insurance on the property, Federal Law authorizes and requires us to purchase the flood insurance for you at your expense.

Flood insurance must cover the lesser of

      The outstanding principal balance of the loan
      The maximum amount of coverage allowed for this type of property under NFIP.

Federal disaster-relief assistance may be available for damages incurred in excess of your flood insurance coverage. TO qualify for Federal Disaster Relief, your community must participate in the NFIP in accordance with NFIP requirements.

Borrower(s) agree to furnish at the borrower(s) expense, a flood insurance policy that meets the lender's requirements on or before closing of the loan.

I/we acknowledge receipt of this notice:

_____   _____
Borrower Signature   Date   Co-Borrower Signature   Date

Pre-Qualification Questionnaire Date: _____

Referral: _____ Phone: _____

Borrower Name: _____ Co-Borrower Name: _____

Home Phone: _____ Other Phone: _____ Best time(s) to call: _____

DOB: _____ SSN: _____ DOB: _____ SSN: _____

May I run a credit report?___ Yes ___ No   May I run a credit report? ___ Yes ___ No

Employer: _____ Employer: _____

Address: _____ Address: _____

Phone: _____ No yrs. ___ Position: _____ Phone: _____ No yrs. ___ Position: _____

Current Address: _____ Check? ___ Yes ___ No

Landlord/Mortgage Holder: _____ Phone: _____

Rent _____ Own ___ No. Yrs: ___ Have you chosen a home to purchase? ___ Yes ___ No Value$_____

___ 1st ___2nd ___Rate/Term Refi ___ C/O Refi ___ Special: _____

Gross Income		Debt	
Borrowers Mthly	$_____	Mortgage/Rental Payment	$_____
Prev Year	$_____	Auto Payment	$_____
Co-Borrowers Mthly	$_____	Auto Payment #2	$_____
Prev Year	$_____	Installment Debt / Type _____	$_____
Other Income _____	$_____	Installment Debt / Type _____	$_____
Other Income _____	$_____	Other _____	$_____
Total Income	$_____	Total Debt	$_____

DTI _____%

Explanation of Credit Situation/Notes: _____

_____

_____

_____

Outcome:

Taken By: _____

L/O: _____

Credit History (12 months)
Borrower

Mortgage Last 12 Months	Consumer Last 12 Months	Bankruptcy NOD/Foreclosure	Charge offs/Judgments
_____ X 30	_____ X 30	Chapter _____	# Filed _____
_____ X 60	_____ X 60	Discharge Date:	$ Amount _____
_____ X 90	_____ X 90	_____	$ to remain open _____
_____ X 120	_____ X 120	Balances: _____	$ to be paid _____
_____ Level	_____ Level	_____ Level	_____ Credit Score

Estimated Credit Level:_____

Credit History (12 months)
Co-Borrower

Mortgage Last 12 Months	Consumer Last 12 Months	Bankruptcy NOD/Foreclosure	Charge offs/Judgments
_____ X 30	_____ X 30	Chapter _____	# Filed _____
_____ X 60	_____ X 60	Discharge Date:	$ Amount _____
_____ X 90	_____ X 90	_____	$ to remain open _____
_____ X 120	_____ X 120	Balances: _____	$ to be paid _____
_____ Level	_____ Level	_____ Level	_____ Credit Score

Estimated Credit Level:_____

DEBT TO INCOME RATIO (DTI%)

Monthly Income

Borrower
$_____ Base Pay/ _____
$_____ Commission/ _____
$_____ Other _____
$_____ Other _____
$_____ Total Monthly Income

Co-Borrower
$_____ Base Pay/ _____
$_____ Commission/ _____
$_____ Other _____
$_____ Other _____
$_____ Total Monthly Income

Combined Monthly Income $_____

Monthly Debt

Borrower
$_____ House/Rent Payment
Automobile Payment
$_____ Credit Card _____
$_____ Credit Card _____
$_____ Credit Card _____
$_____ Personal Loan _____
$_____ Other_____
$_____ Other_____
$_____ Total Monthly Debt

Co-Borrower
$_____ House/Rent Payment(factor once) $_____
$_____ Automobile Payment
$_____ Credit Card _____
$_____ Credit Card _____
$_____ Credit Card _____
$_____ Personal Loan _____
$_____ Other_____
$_____ Other_____
$_____ Total Monthly Debt

Combined Monthly Debt $_____

Take combined debt $_____ (factor each debt only once – if it is a joint debt list under the primary income earner only) and divide by the combined income $_____. The percentage _____% is your monthly debt-to-income ratio. This number should be below the maximum set forth in the loan matrix for the product level you have chosen for your borrowers. You can change the housing expense ratio to customize the ratios to fit your matrix. Just remember to alter the purchase price on your application to match or your underwriting team will decline the loan package for excessive ratios.

CREDIT REPORT AUTHORIZATION AND RELEASE

Authorization is hereby granted to _____ to obtain a standard factual data credit report through a credit-reporting agency chosen by the
_____.

My signature below authorizes the release to the credit-reporting agency a copy of my credit application, and authorizes the credit-reporting agency to obtain information regarding my employment, savings accounts, and outstanding credit accounts (mortgages, auto loans, personal loans, charge cards, credit unions, etc.) Authorization is further granted to the reporting agency to use a Photostatted reproduction of this authorization if necessary to obtain any information regarding the above-mentioned information.

Applicants hereby request a copy of the credit report with any possible derogatory information be sent to the address of present residence, and holds _____ and any credit reporting organization harmless in so mailing the copy requested.

Any reproduction of this credit authorization and release made by reliable means (for example: photocopy or facsimile is considered an original.

_____

Borrower's Signature
Date:
SSN:

_____

Borrower's Signature
Date:
SSN:

_____

Borrower's Signature
Date:
SSN:

_____

Borrower's Signature
Date:
SSN:

CREDIT DENIAL LETTER

Dear Applicant:

Thank you for your recent mortgage application. Your request for a loan was carefully considered, and we regret that we are unable to approve your application at this time.

This decision is based on the following factor(s):

__ Insufficient income to meet our minimum requirements
__ Insufficient income to sustain payments on the amount of credit requested
__ Income could not be verified
__ Employment history is not of sufficient length to qualify
__ Employment history could not be verified
__ Credit history of timely payments is unsatisfactory
__ Credit history could not be verified
__ Lack of sufficient credit references
__ Lack of acceptable types of credit references
__ Current obligations are excessive in relationship to income
__ Other _____

We will keep your application on file and look forward to working with you in the near future when your situation has changed.

STACKING ORDER CHECKLIST

____ Loan Coversheet

____ Loan Submission Form

____ Stacking Order Checklist

____ Full 1008 or underwriting transmittal summary

____ Full, signed 1003 application

____ Purpose of Refinance Letter if applicable to the transaction

____ Credit Report

____ Credit Supplements if any are applicable to the loan file

____ Letter of explanation regarding any questionable or derogatory item on the credit report

____ A verification of mortgage or rent form or 12 months cancelled rent checks

____ All Bankruptcy Discharge Documentation if it is applicable to the transaction

____ A Divorce Decree if it is applicable to the transaction

____ A verification of deposit if checking or savings funds will be used toward the funds to close

____ A breakdown of the source of funds for closing

____ Gift letters signed by donors if they are applicable to the transaction

____ Verification of employment forms

____ Most Recent 30 Days Pay stubs

____ W-2's or full tax returns from preceding two years

____ Documentation of other income if it is applicable to the transaction

____ Sales Agreement including all pages and addendums

_____ Rental or Lease Agreements if they are applicable to the transaction

_____ Appraisal Report with original photographs

_____ Preliminary Title Report

_____ Title Commitment

_____ Copy of any exiting note if the transaction is a refinance transaction

_____ Escrow or funding instructions

_____ Original Good Faith Estimate and Truth in Lending disclosures

_____ ECOA, Fair Lending, and other Applicable Disclosures

_____ Broker Agreements

_____ And any other documentation specific to the loan file.

6:1 Sample Form – Underwriting Submission

UNDERWRITING SUBMISSION FORM

FAX _____

Date: _____	Broker Name: _____
Broker Code: _____	Broker Contact: _____
Broker Phone: _____	Broker FAX: _____

If loan is locked – provide Loan Number: _____

Borrower's Name: _____

Co-Borrower's Name: _____

Purchase Price: $_____   LTV: _____%   CLTV: _____%

Appraised Value: $_____   Loan Amount: $_____

LOAN PRODUCT	PURPOSE	OCCUPANCY	PROPERTY TYPE
__ 30 Yr Fixed	__ Purchase	__ Primary Residence	__ SFR
__ 15 Yr Fixed	__ Refi No Cash	__ Second Home	__ 2 Family
__ FHA/VA	__ Refi Cash out	__ Investment	__ 3-4 Family
__ FNMA Fallout			__ Condo/PUD
__ Lite Doc			
__ Other _____			

DOCUMENTATION
__ Signed 1003
__ Signed Good Faith
__ Pre-qualification 1003
__ Consent for Credit Check
__ Credit Report
__ VOR/VOM
__ W2/Tax Returns
__ Pay Stubs
__ Source of Funds
__ Other _____

_____

REQUEST INFORMATION: _____

_____

_____

_____

_____

Submission Sheet

DATE SUBMITTED: _____ ACCOUNT EXECUTIVE: _____
BROKER: _____
ADDRESS: _____
CONTACT: _____ PHONE: _____ FAX: _____

```
┌─────────────────────────────────────────────────────────────────────┐
│                      BORROWER/LOAN INFORMATION                        │
│                                                                       │
│ BORROWER: _____ SSN: _____       │
│ CO-BORROWER: _____ SSN: _____       │
│ PROPERTY ADDRESS: _____           │
│                                                                       │
│ ( ) Owner Occupied      ( ) Purchase     ( ) Full Doc      ( ) SFR    │
│ ( ) 2nd Home            ( ) Refinance     ( ) Lite Doc     ( ) Townhouse│
│ ( ) Non-owner Occupied                    ( ) Stated Doc   ( ) _____ │
│                                                                       │
│ LOAN AMOUNT: $_____    PROGRAM: _____             │
│ APPRAISED VALUE: $_____    RATE: _____ TERM: _____          │
│ SALES PRICE: $ _____    LTV: _____ CLTV: _____           │
└─────────────────────────────────────────────────────────────────────┘
```

BROKER'S FEES

ORIGINATION ____%   _____
REBATE ____%   _____
PROCESSING   _____
APPRAISAL   _____
CREDIT REPORT   _____
                           _____
_____   _____
_____   _____

```
┌─────────────────────────────────────────────────────────────────────┐
│                        FILE STACKING ORDER                            │
│ __ SUBMISSION FORM            __ VOE'S                                 │
│ __ TYPED 1008                 __ CURRENT PAYSTUBS                      │
│ __ TYPED 1003                 __ LAST 2 YEARS W-2'S/1099'S             │
│ __ HANDWRITTEN 1003           __ YTD PROFIT & LOSS STMT (SELF-EMP)     │
│ __ PURPOSE LETTER             __ LAST 2 YEARS 1040'2                   │
│ __ CREDIT EXPLANATION         __ LAST 2 YEARS 1120/1065               │
│ __ CREDIT REPORT              __ APPRAISAL WITH ORIGINAL PHOTOS        │
│ __ VOM/12 MONTH RENT CKS      __ PRELIMINAY TITLE                      │
│ __ BK SCHEDULE & DIS          __ COPY OF EXISTING NOTE                 │
│ __ DIVORCE DECREE             __ EXECUTED SALES CONTRACT               │
│ __ VOD                        __ BROKERS DISCLOSURES                   │
└─────────────────────────────────────────────────────────────────────┘
```

ORIGINAL PACKAGE REQUIRED

6:2 Sample Form – Submission Sheet

REQUEST FOR VERIFICATION OF EMPLOYMENT

Instructions	Lender – Complete items 1 through 7. Have applicant complete item 8. Forward directly to employer named in item 1.
	Employer – Please complete either Part II or Part III as applicable. Complete Part IV and return directly to lender named in item 2.
	This form is to be transmitted directly to the lender and is not to be transmitted through the applicant or any other party.

Part I – Request

1. To (Name and address of employer)	2. From (Name and address of Lender)

I certify that this verification has been sent directly to the employer and ahs not passed through the hands of the applicant or any other interested party.

2. Signature of Lender	4. Title	4. Date	6. Lender's Number (Optional)

I have applied for a mortgage loan and stated that I am now or was formerly employed by you. My signature below authorizes verification of this information.

7. Name and Address of Applicant (include employee or badge number)	8. Signature of Applicant

Part II – Verification of Present Employment

9. Applicant's Date of Employment	10. Present Position	11. Probability of Continued Employment

12A. Current Gross Base Pay (enter Amount and Check Period) __ Annual __ Hourly __ Monthly __ Other (specify) $ _____ __ Weekly	13 For Military Personnel Only		14. If Overtime or Bonus is Applicable Is Its Continuance Likely? Overtime __ Yes __ No Bonus __ Yes __ No 15. If paid hourly – average hours per week
	Pay Grade		
	Type	Monthly Amount	
	Base Pay	$	

Type	Year to Date	Past Year 20_	Past Year 20_	Rations	$	16. Date of applicant's next pay increase
Base Pay	$	$	$	Flight or Hazard	$	
Overtime	$	$	$	Clothing	$	17. Projected amount of next pay increase
				Quarters	$	
Commissions	$	$	$	Pro Pay	$	18. Date of applicant's last pay increase
Bonus	$	$	$	Overseas or Combat	$	19. Amount of last pay increase
Total	$	$	$	Variable Housing Allowance	$	

20. Remarks (If employee was off work for any length of time, please indicate time period and reason)

Part III Verification of Previous Employment

21. Date Hired	23. Salary/Wage at Termination Per (Year) (Month) (Week) Base _____ Overtime _____ Commissions _____ Bonus _____
22. Date Terminated	
24. Reason for Leaving	25. Position Held

Part IV – Authorized Signature

26. Signature of Employer	27. Title (please print or type)	28. Date
29. Print or type named signed in item 26	30. Phone No.	

6:3 Sample Form – Verification of Employment – HUD Release

REQUEST FOR VERIFICATION OF RENT OR MORTGAGE

Instructions   Lender – Complete items 1 through 8. Have applicant complete item 9. Forward directly to landlord named in item 1.
Landlord Creditor – Please complete Items 10 through 18 and return directly to lender named in item 2.
This form is to be transmitted directly to the lender and is not to be transmitted through the applicant or any other party.

Part I – Request

1. To (Name and address of Landlord Creditor)	2. From (Name and address of Lender)

I certify that this verification has been sent directly to the landlord/creditor and ahs not passed through the hands of the applicant or any other interested party.

2. Signature of Lender	4. Title	4. Date	6. Lender's Number (Optional)

7. Information To Be Verified

Property Address	Account in the Name of	Account Number
	__ Mortgage __ Rental __ Land Contract	

I have applied for a mortgage loan. My signature below authorizes verification of mortgage or rent information.

8. Name and Address of Applicant(s)	9. Signature of Applicant(s) X X

Part II – To Be Completed by the Landlord/Creditor

We have received an application for a loan from the above, to whom we understand you rent or have extended a loan. In addition to the information requested below, please furnish us with any information you might have that will assist us in processing the loan.

__ Rental Account	__ Mortgage Account	__ Land Contract
10. Tenant Rented from _____ to _____ Amount of rent $_____ per _____ Number of late payments _____ Is account satisfactory? __ Yes __ No	11. Date account opened _____ Original contract amount $_____ Current account balance $_____ Monthly Payment (P&I) $_____ Payment with T&I $_____ Is account current? __ Yes __ No Was loan assumed? __ Yes __ No Satisfactory account? __ Yes __ No	12. Interest Rate _____ % __ Fixed __ ARM __ FHA __ VA __ CONV __ Other Next pay date _____ No. of late payments _____ No. of late charges _____ Owner of First Mortgage _____

Payment History for the previous 12 months must be provided n order to comply with secondary mortgage market requirements.

13. Additional information which may be of assistance in determination of credit worthiness

14. Signature of Landlord/Creditor Representative	15. Title (please print or type)	Date

17. Please print or type name signed in Item 14

6:4 Sample Form – Verification of Rent or Mortgage – HUD Release

REQUEST FOR VERIFICATION OF DEPOSIT

Privacy Act Notice: This information is to be used by the agency collecting it or its assignees in determining whether you qualify as a prospective mortgagor under its program. It will not be disclosed outside the agency except as required and permitted by law. You do not have to provide this information, but if you do not your application for approval as a prospective mortgagor or borrower may be delayed or rejected. The information requested in this form is authorized by Title 38, USC. Chapter 37 (if VA); by 12 USC, Section 1701 et. Seq (if HUD/FHA); by 42 USC, Section 1452b (if HUD/CPD); and Title 42 USC, 1471 et. Seq., or 7 USC. 1971 et. Deq. (if USDA/FmHA).

Instructions   Lender – Complete items 1 through 8. Have applicant complete item 9. Forward directly to depository named in item 1.
Depository – Please complete Items 10 through 18 and return DIRECTLY to lender named in item 2.
This form is to be transmitted directly to the lender and is not to be transmitted through the applicant or any other party.

PART I - REQUEST

1. To (Name and address of depository)	2. From (Name and address of Lender)

I certify that this verification has been sent directly to the bank or depository and ahs not passed through the hands of the applicant or any other interested party.

2. Signature of Lender	4. Title	4. Date	6. Lender's Number (Optional)

7. Information To Be Verified

Type of Account	Account in Name of	Account Number	Balance
			$
			$
			$

To Depository: I/We have applied for a mortgage loan and stated in my financial statement that the balance on deposit with you is as shown above. You are authorized to verify this information and to supply the lender identified above with the information requested in Items 10 through 13. Your response is solely a matter of courtesy for which no responsibility is attached to your institution or any of your officers.

8. Name and Address of Applicant(s)	9. Signature of Applicant(s)

PART II – VERIFICATION OF DEPOSITORY To Be Completed By Depository

10. Deposit Accounts of Applicant(s)

Type of Account	Account in Name of	Account Number	Balance
			$
			$
			$

11. Loans Outstanding To Applicants

Loan Number	Date of Loan	Original Amount	Current Balance	Installments (Monthly/Quarterly)		Secured By	Number of Late Payments
		$	$	$	per		
		$	$	$	per		
		$	$	$	per		

12. Please include any additional information which may be of assistance in determination of credit worthiness. (Please include information on loans paid-in-full in Item 11 above)

13. If the name(s) on the account(s) differ from those listed in Item 7, please supply the name(s) on the account(s) as reflected by your records.

PART III – Authorized Signature – Federal statutes provide severe penalty for any fraud, intentional misrepresentation, or criminal connivance or conspiracy purposed to influence the issuance of any guaranty or insurance by the VA Secretary, the U.S.D.A., FmHA/FHA Commissioner, or the HUD/CPD Assistant Secretary.

14. Signature of Depository Representative	15. Title (please print or type)	16. Date
17. Please print or type name signed in item 14	18. Phone No.	

6:5 Sample Form – Verification of Deposit – HUD Release

Appraisal Request Form

DATE: _____   FROM: _____

TO: _____   FAX: _____

PURCHASE/REFINANCE/OTHER   FHA/VA/RURAL HOUSING/CONVENTIONAL

APPLICANT/BORROWERS: _____ PHONE: _____

REAL ESTATE AGENT: _____ PHONE:
_____

CONTACT INFORMATION: _____

PROPERTY INFORMATION: _____

ESTIMATED VALUE   _____   SALES PRICE: _____

LENDER'S NAME: _____

PAYMENT OPTION: _____

ADDITIONAL COMMENTS: _____

ITEMS ATTACHED: ___ Sales Agreement Page 1
                              ___ Sales Agreement Page 2
                              ___ Original Purchase Document
                              ___ Previous Appraisal
                              ___ Other: _____

6:6 Sample Form – Appraisal Request Form

Title Request Form

DATE: _____   FROM: _____

TO: _____   FAX: _____

Borrower Name: _____

Phone Number: _____ SS#_____ SS#_____

Mailing Address: _____

Property Address: _____

Proposed Lender: _____   Loan Amount: _____

Purchase ____   Refinance ____   2nd Mortgage ____   Prepared by: _____

Current Owners: _____

Address: _____

Phone Number: _____ SS#_____ SS#_____

Estimated Close Date: _____
Purchase Price: $_____   Loan Amount: $_____
Attachments:

     1003
     Sales Agreement

     _____
     _____

6:7 Sample Form – Title Request Form

Request for Homeowners Insurance Quote

Borrower : _____Co-Borrower Name: _____

DOB: _____ DOB:_____

SSN: _____ SSN: _____

Mailing Address: _____

Home Phone: _____ Best Time to Call: _____

Property Address: _____

Value: _____ Sales Price: _____

Payment to be made: _____ Prior to Close _____ At Close

Expected Close Date: _____ Binder Needed By: _____

Proposed Lender: _____

Additional Comments: _____

Attachments:

_____1003
_____Credit Report
_____Sales Agreement
_____Appraisal
_____

_____

OCCUPANCY DECLARATIONS

Lender:

RE: Loan No:
        PROPERTY ADDRESS:

The undersigned Borrower of the above described property does hereby declare, under penalty of perjury, as follows:

1.   Borrower shall occupy, establish, and use the Property as Borrowers principal residence within sixty days after execution of the Security Instrument and shall continue to occupy the property as Borrower's principal residence for at least one year after the date of occupancy unless Lender otherwise agrees in writing, which consent shall not be unreasonably withheld, or unless extenuating circumstances exist which are beyond the Borrower's control.

        You are hereby informed that Lender from time to time makes spot checks for owner occupancy on properties upon which we have secured a mortgage.

        Between the first and thirteenth day, after close of escrow, occupancy may be checked more than once. If after this check Lender is to believe that you never intended to occupy the subject as your primary residence, we may choose to call your note due and payable or increase your note rate by 100 basis points, in accordance with the applicable sections itemized on your note and Security Instrument and allowable by law.

2.   Borrower shall be in default, if during the loan application process, gave materially false or inaccurate information or statements to Lender (or failed to provide Lender with material information) in connection with the loan evidenced by the Note, including, but not limited to, representations concerning Borrower's occupancy of the Property as a Principal residence.

3.   The Lender has the right to foreclose on the loan under the terms of the Security Instrument if items 1 or 2 above are violated.

4.   Should Borrower's intention change prior to close of transaction, then it is agreed that the Lender will be immediately notified of that fact.

5.   Borrower understands that without this declaration of intention, Lender may not make the loan in connection with the property.

I DECLARE, UNDER PENALTY OF PERJURY, THAT THE FOREGOING DECLARATION IS TRUE AND CORRECT.

6:11 Sample Extraction – Occupancy Declaration – HUD Release

FEE DISCLOSURE

APPLICANT(S) NAME AND ADDRESS	MORTGAGE BANKER/BROKER NAME AND ADDRESS
PROPERTY ADDRESS	TYPE OF LOAN

Today you have submitted a mortgage loan application to the Mortgage Banker or Broker listed above. All fees paid by you are nonrefundable. State law requires that the following information be disclosed to you.

The Mortgage Banker or Broker is required to refund all fees paid by an applicant borrower, other than those fees paid by the Mortgage Banker or Broker to a third party, when a mortgage loan is not produced within the time specified by the Mortgage Banker or Broker at the rate, term and overall cost agreed to by the borrower.

However, this provision shall not apply when the failure to produce a loan is due solely to the borrower's negligence, borrower's refusal to accept and close on a loan commitment or borrower's refusal or inability to provide information necessary for processing the loan, including, but not limited to, employment verifications and verifications of deposit.

This disclosure does not constitute approval of your loan or a commitment to make a loan to you.

6:11 Sample Extraction – Fee Disclosure – HUD Release

www.ingramcontent.com/pod-product-compliance
Lightning Source LLC
Chambersburg PA
CBHW080051280326
41934CB00014B/3280